MR 25 '02	DATE DUE		
AP 19 '02 NOV 2 9 '11			
MY 07 '02			
OC 04 '02			
FE 04 '03			
FE 18 '03			
AP 13 '05			
MY 09 '05			
FEB 2 5 '08			
APR 2 2 '08			
OCT 2 2 '09			
FEB 0 3 '11			

Using and Understanding Maps

The Military World

Consulting Editor
Scott E. Morris
College of Mines and Earth Resources
University of Idaho

Chelsea House Publishers
New York   Philadelphia

This Publication was designed, edited and computer generated by
Lovell Johns Limited
10 Hanborough Business Park
Long Hanborough
Witney
Oxon, England OX8 8LH

General Editor and Project Manager   Alison Dickinson
Research and Text   Gill Lloyd

The contents of this volume are based on the latest data available at the
time of publication.

Map credit: *Antarctica source map prepared at 1:20,000 by the British
Antarctic Survey Mapping and Geographic Information Centre, 1990*

Cover credit: *United Nations Photo*

Printed in Mexico

3 5 7 9 8 6 4 2

Library of Congress Cataloging in Publication Data

The Military world/editorial consultant, Scott Morris:
        p. cm.—(Using and understanding maps)
        Includes glossary and index/gazetteer.
        Includes bibliographical references.
        Summary: Eighteen map spreads show the military strengths of
        countries and alliances throughout the world.
        ISBN 0-7910-1808-3. — ISBN 0-7910-1821-0 (pbk.)
        1. Military geography—Maps. [1. Military geography—Maps,
        2. Atlases.]
        I. Morris, Scott Edward. II. Chelsea House Publishers. III Series.
        G1046.R1M5 1993 <G&M>
        355.4' 7' 0223 — dc20   92-22286
                                                       CIP
                                                       MAP AC

Introduction

We inhabit a fascinating and mysterious planet where the earth's physical features, life-forms, and the diversity of human culture conspire to produce a breathtaking environment. We don't have to travel very far to see and experience the wealth of this diverse planet; in fact, we don't have to travel at all. Everywhere images of the world are abundantly available in books, newspapers, magazines, movies, television, and the arts. We could say that *everywhere* one looks, our world is a brilliant moving tapestry of shapes, colors, and textures, and our experience of its many messages — whether in our travels or simply by gazing out into our own backyards — is what we call reality.

Geography is the study of a portion of that reality. More so, it is the study of how the physical and biological components (rocks, animals, plants, and people) of our planet are distributed and how they are interconnected. Geographers seek to describe and to explain the physical patterns that have evolved on the earth and also to discover the significance in the ways they have evolved. To do this, geographers rely on maps.

Maps can be powerful images. They convey selective information about vast areas of an overwhelmingly cluttered world. The cartographer, or mapmaker, must carefully choose the theme of a map, that is, what it will show, knowing that a good map will convey the essence of information while at the same time making the information easy to comprehend.

This volume and its companions in UNDERSTANDING AND USING MAPS are about the planet we call earth and the maps we use to find our way along its peaks and valleys. Each volume displays map images that reveal how the world is arranged according to a specific theme such as population, industries or the endangered world. The maps in each volume are accompanied by an interesting collection of facts — some are rather obvious, others are oddities. Yet all are meant to be informative.

Along with a wealth of facts, there are explanations of the various attributes and phenomena depicted by the maps. This information is provided to better understand the significance of the maps as well as to demonstrate how the many themes relate.

Names for places are essential to geographers. To study the world without devising names for places would be extremely difficult. But geographers also know that names are in no way permanent; place names change as people change. The recent reunification of Germany and the breakup of what was the Soviet Union — events that seem colossal from the perspective of socioeconomics — to geographers are simply events that require the drawing or erasing of one or a few boundaries and the renaming of one or several land masses. The geographer is constantly reminded that the world is in flux; a map is always in danger of being rendered obsolete by a turn in current events.

Because the world is dynamic, it continues to captivate the mind and stimulate the imagination. USING AND UNDERSTANDING MAPS presents the world as it is today, with the reservation that any dramatic rearrangement of land and people is likely, indeed inevitable, thus requiring the making of a new map. In this way maps are themselves a part of the evolutionary process.

Scott E. Morris

The Military World

It goes without saying that the modern world is complicated. Peoples of different races, ethnic origins, religions, languages, livelihoods, and national allegiances are in daily contact with each other. Often people with different ideas, cultures, and histories inhabit the same country. Conflicts between these peoples have occurred frequently throughout history.

Governments have found it necessary to form and maintain armed forces. These armed forces have served as protection from outside aggression, as well as a means of keeping the peace within the country's borders. These forces also have an offensive capability, and history is full of examples of one country invading another.

Geography once exercised a fundamental influence over the military world. Before advanced weapons were developed, many a battle was won or lost by utilizing (or neglecting) the advantages of the landscape. Oceans presented barriers to the movement of troops, until navies arose to control the waterways. Mountains provided protection from invaders. Armies could not march very far from the areas where their food was grown. But in this age of satellite communications, ballistic missiles with nuclear warheads, and supersonice aircraft, distance and topography no longer offer much protection. The military world reaches everywhere.

It is difficult to logically explain how the military world has reached its present state of development. The maps and statistics in this volume will amaze you and make you think. The cost of the military world, both in terms of the human lives lost throughout history, and the financial resources dedicated to military forces and machines, is staggering. Modern warfare is waged with sophisticated computers and extraordinarily expensive weaponry. In 1989, the world spent $1.1 trillion on armaments. Modern nations routinely spend far more money on their military organizations than they do on education or health care. And still more expensive weapons are designed every year.

There are signs of hope. The dissolution of the Soviet Union and the realignment of eastern Europe has brought the cold war to a virtual end. The end of international tensions between the superpowers has removed the underlying reason for the arms race. Many people are now demanding that the money committed to defense be channeled into more productive and humanitarian uses. In regions still experiencing conflicts, international peace-keeping forces are being deployed to work for cease-fire agreements and negotiated settlements. Economic sanctions and political pressures are applied to countries that violate international law. These are all indications that our civilization may be maturing to the point where armaments and deadly force are not required to solve disagreements.

The military world presented in this volume illustrates yet another dimension to human culture. It is another layer of the mosaic that is the human geography of our planet. One can only hope that the military world will be much smaller in the future.

Scott E. Morris

A legend lists and explains the symbols and colors used on the map. It is called a legend because it tells the story of a map. It is important to read the map legend to find out exactly what the symbols mean because some symbols do not look like what they represent. For example, a dot stands for a town.
Every map in this atlas has a legend on it.

This legend lists and explains the colors and symbols used on the map on that page only.
The legend on the left, below, shows examples of the colors used on the maps in all the atlases in this series. Below this is a list of all symbols used on the maps in all the atlases in this series.
The legend on the right, below, is an example of a legend used in the physical atlas.

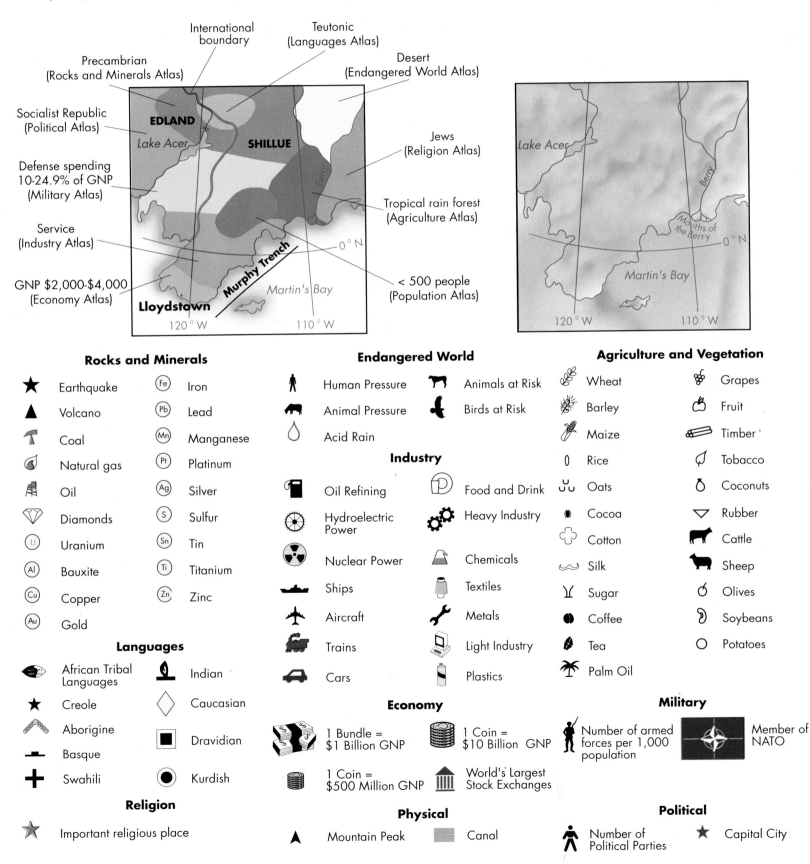

Rocks and Minerals

★ Earthquake
▲ Volcano
⚒ Coal
🝆 Natural gas
🛢 Oil
◈ Diamonds
Ⓤ Uranium
Ⓐⓛ Bauxite
Ⓒⓤ Copper
Ⓐⓤ Gold

Ⓕⓔ Iron
Ⓟⓑ Lead
Ⓜⓝ Manganese
Ⓟⓣ Platinum
Ⓐⓖ Silver
Ⓢ Sulfur
Ⓢⓝ Tin
Ⓣⓘ Titanium
Ⓩⓝ Zinc

Languages

👁 African Tribal Languages
★ Creole
🪃 Aborigine
— Basque
✝ Swahili

🕯 Indian
◇ Caucasian
◼ Dravidian
◉ Kurdish

Religion

✩ Important religious place

Endangered World

🧍 Human Pressure
🐄 Animal Pressure
💧 Acid Rain

🐂 Animals at Risk
🦅 Birds at Risk

Industry

⛽ Oil Refining
⚙ Hydroelectric Power
☢ Nuclear Power
🚢 Ships
✈ Aircraft
🚂 Trains
🚗 Cars

Ⓟ Food and Drink
⚙ Heavy Industry
🔺 Chemicals
🧵 Textiles
🔧 Metals
💻 Light Industry
🧴 Plastics

Economy

💵 1 Bundle = $1 Billion GNP
🪙 1 Coin = $500 Million GNP

🪙 1 Coin = $10 Billion GNP
🏛 World's Largest Stock Exchanges

Physical

▲ Mountain Peak
▬ Canal

Agriculture and Vegetation

🌾 Wheat
🌿 Barley
🌽 Maize
0 Rice
Ⴑ Oats
● Cocoa
❀ Cotton
〰 Silk
Ⴘ Sugar
● Coffee
🍃 Tea
🌴 Palm Oil

🍇 Grapes
🍎 Fruit
🪵 Timber
🍂 Tobacco
🥥 Coconuts
▽ Rubber
🐄 Cattle
🐑 Sheep
🫒 Olives
🫘 Soybeans
O Potatoes

Military

🪖 Number of armed forces per 1,000 population
✛ Member of NATO

Political

🧍 Number of Political Parties
★ Capital City

World Physical

This page is a physical map of the world. It indicates where the major physical features — such as mountain ranges, plains, deserts, lakes, and rivers — are in the world. As the world is very large, the map has to be drawn at a very small scale in order to fit onto a page. This map is drawn at a scale so that 1 inch on the map, at the equator, equals 1,840 miles on the ground.

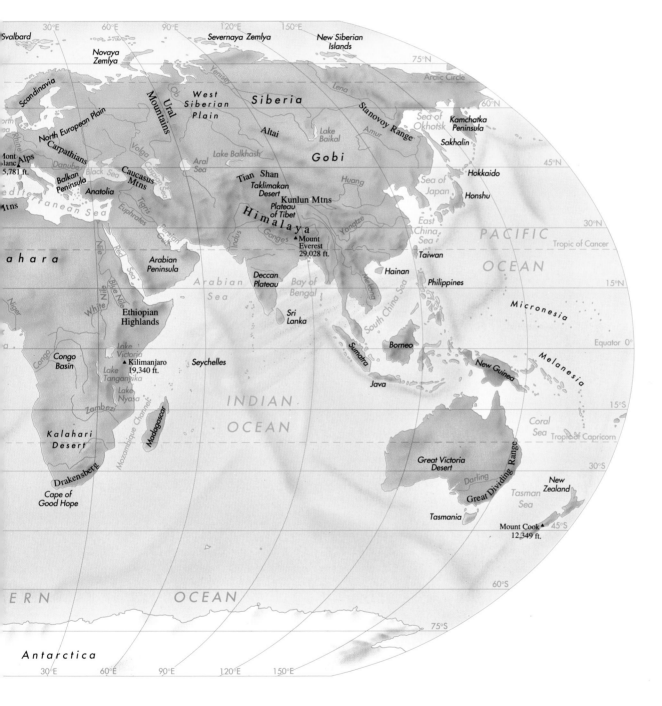

Svalbard

Novaya
Zemlya

Severnaya Zemlya

New Siberian
Islands

75°N

Arctic Circle

Scandinavia

North European Plain

Ural
Mountains

Ob

West
Siberian
Plain

Siberia

Yenisey

Lena

Stanovoy Range

60°N

Sea of
Okhotsk

Kamchatka
Peninsula

Sakhalin

North
Sea

Rhine

Carpathians

Alps

Mont
Blanc
5,781 ft.

Danube

Volga

Altai

Lake
Baikal

Amur

Gobi

45°N

Hokkaido

Sea of
Japan

Honshu

Balkan
Peninsula

Black Sea

Caucasus
Mtns

Aral
Sea

Caspian Sea

Tian Shan

Taklimakan
Desert

Huang

Anatolia

Mediterranean Sea

Mtns

Tigris

Euphrates

Persian Gulf

Kunlun Mtns
Plateau
of Tibet

Himalaya

Mount
Everest
29,028 ft.

Yangtze

East
China
Sea

PACIFIC

30°N

Tropic of Cancer

ahara

Nile

Red Sea

Arabian
Peninsula

Indus

Ganges

Taiwan

OCEAN

Arabian
Sea

Deccan
Plateau

Bay of
Bengal

Hainan

Philippines

Mekong

15°N

Micronesia

Blue Nile

White

Ethiopian
Highlands

Sri
Lanka

South China Sea

Equator 0°

Niger

Lake
Victoria

Kilimanjaro
19,340 ft.

Seychelles

Borneo

New Guinea

Melanesia

Congo

Congo
Basin

Lake
Tanganyika

Sumatra

Java

15°S

INDIAN

Lake
Nyasa

Zambezi

Mozambique Channel

Madagascar

OCEAN

Coral
Sea

Tropic of Capricorn

Kalahari
Desert

Great Victoria
Desert

Great Dividing Range

30°S

Drakensberg

Darling

New
Zealand

Cape of
Good Hope

Great Dividing Range

Tasman
Sea

Tasmania

Mount Cook
12,349 ft.

45°S

60°S

ERN

OCEAN

75°S

Antarctica

30°E   60°E   90°E   120°E   150°E

World Key Map

Africa, Northern 10-11

Algeria
Benin
Burkina Faso
Cameroon
Cape Verde
Central African Republic
Chad
Djibouti
Egypt
Ethiopia
Gambia
Ghana
Guinea
Guinea-Bissau
Ivory Coast
Liberia
Libya
Mali
Mauritania
Morocco
Niger
Nigeria
Senegal
Sierra Leone
Somalia
Sudan
Togo
Tunisia
Western Sahara

Africa, Southern 12-13

Angola
Botswana
Burundi
Comoros
Congo
Equatorial Guinea
Gabon
Kenya
Lesotho
Madagascar
Malawi
Mauritius
Mozambique
Namibia
Rwanda

São Tomé & Príncipe
Seychelles
South Africa
Swaziland
Tanzania
Uganda
Zaire
Zambia
Zimbabwe

America, Central 14-15

Antigua & Barbuda
Bahamas
Barbados
Belize
Costa Rica
Cuba
Dominica

Dominican Republic
El Salvador
Grenada
Guatemala
Haiti
Honduras
Jamaica

Mexico
Nicaragua
Panama
St Kitts - Nevis
St Lucia
St Vincent
Trinidad & Tobago

**Canada
26-27**

**United States
of America
40-41**

**Central
America
14-15**

**Oceania
38-39**

**South America
16-17**

Canada 26-27

Canada

Commonwealth of Independent States 28-29

Armenia
Azerbaijan
Estonia
Georgia
Kazakhstan
Kirghizstan
Latvia
Lithuania
Moldova
Russian Federation

Tajikistan
Turkmenistan
Ukraine
Uzbekhistan

Europe 30-31

Albania
Bosnia & Herzegovina
Bulgaria
Croatia
Czechoslovakia
Finland
Greece
Hungary
Iceland
Norway

Poland
Romania
Slovenia
Sweden
Yugoslavia

Europe, Western 32-33

Andorra
Austria
Belgium
Denmark
France
Germany
Ireland
Italy
Liechtenstein
Luxembourg

Malta
Monaco
Netherlands
Portugal
San Marino
Spain
Switzerland
United Kingdom
Vatican City

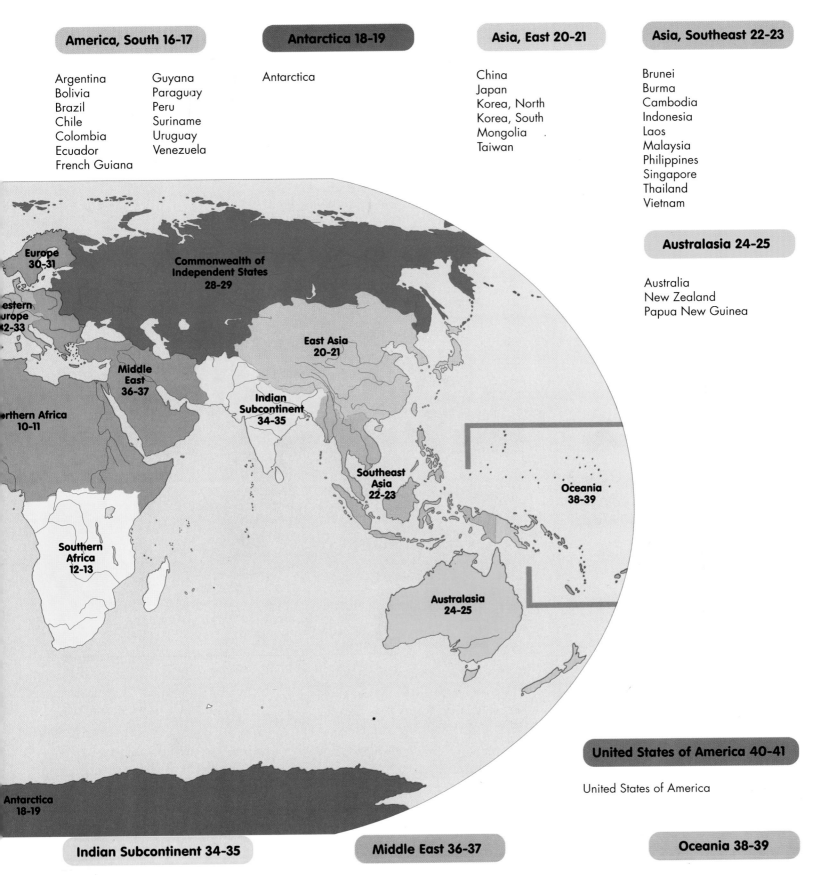

America, South 16-17

Argentina   Guyana
Bolivia   Paraguay
Brazil   Peru
Chile   Suriname
Colombia   Uruguay
Ecuador   Venezuela
French Guiana

Antarctica 18-19

Antarctica

Asia, East 20-21

China
Japan
Korea, North
Korea, South
Mongolia   .
Taiwan

Asia, Southeast 22-23

Brunei
Burma
Cambodia
Indonesia
Laos
Malaysia
Philippines
Singapore
Thailand
Vietnam

Australasia 24-25

Australia
New Zealand
Papua New Guinea

United States of America 40-41

United States of America

Indian Subcontinent 34-35

Afghanistan
Bangladesh
Bhutan
India
Maldives
Nepal
Pakistan
Sri Lanka

Middle East 36-37

Bahrain   Saudi Arabia
Cyprus   Syria
Iran   Turkey
Iraq   United Arab Emirates
Israel   Yemen
Jordan
Kuwait
Lebanon
Oman
Qatar

Oceania 38-39

Fiji
Kiribati
Nauru
Solomon Islands
Tonga
Tuvalu
Vanuatu
Western Samoa

Regional tensions are still very much part of this area, despite attempts to further economic cooperation. The war in the Western Sahara has put a strain on Morocco, while the wars in the Sudan and in Ethiopia have had devastating consequences.

Total War

One in which a nation uses all its human resources and weapons. In such wars civilians as well as military people take part. World Wars I and II were total wars.

Limited War

Limited wars are those in which the weapons used and the targets attacked are limited by the nations involved. Limited war has come to mean a war in which neither side uses atomic weapons.

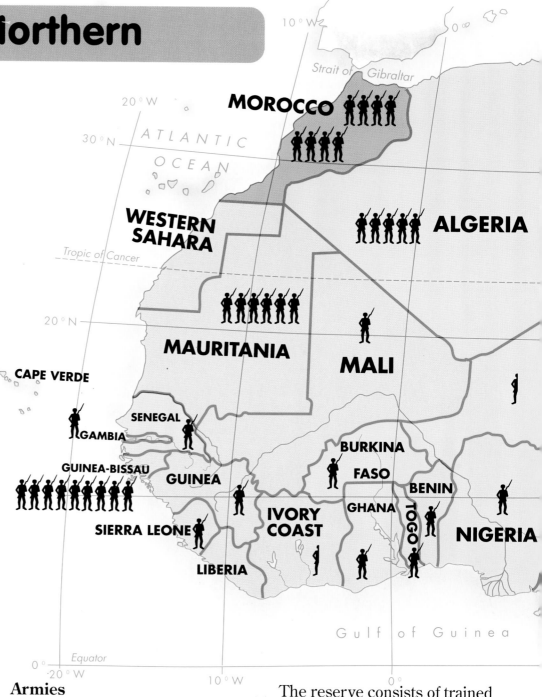

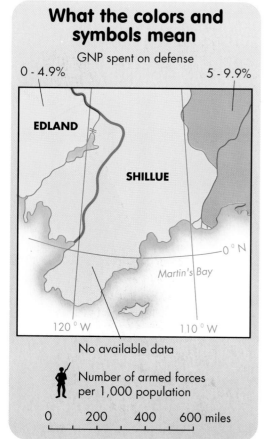

What the colors and symbols mean

GNP spent on defense

0 - 4.9%   5 - 9.9%

EDLAND

SHILLUE

Martin's Bay

0°N

120°W   110°W

No available data

Number of armed forces per 1,000 population

0   200   400   600 miles

Armies

Practically every nation has an army, the part of the armed forces that is trained to fight on land. Armies consist of soldiers and their weapons and equipment ; depending on the size and sophistication of the armed forces, they may also consist of armored tanks, artillery, and support troops who deal with transportation, medical care, and similar important roles.

Most countries distinguish between their regular army and their army reserve. The regular army is made up of professional soldiers who are constantly being trained and are always ready for combat.

The reserve consists of trained civilians who can be called up at any time. Countries have different ways of recruiting their forces. Some use only volunteers; others use a military draft, or conscription, which selects certain individuals for army duty; still others require all qualified men and women to serve.

Nearly all highly developed nations have well-equipped troops and the latest tanks and infantry. The most powerful armies also have fleets of helicopters, personnel carriers, and guided missiles. The top armies combine great striking power with high mobility. The armies that are considered the most powerful are: the Chinese army, with about 2 million troops on active service

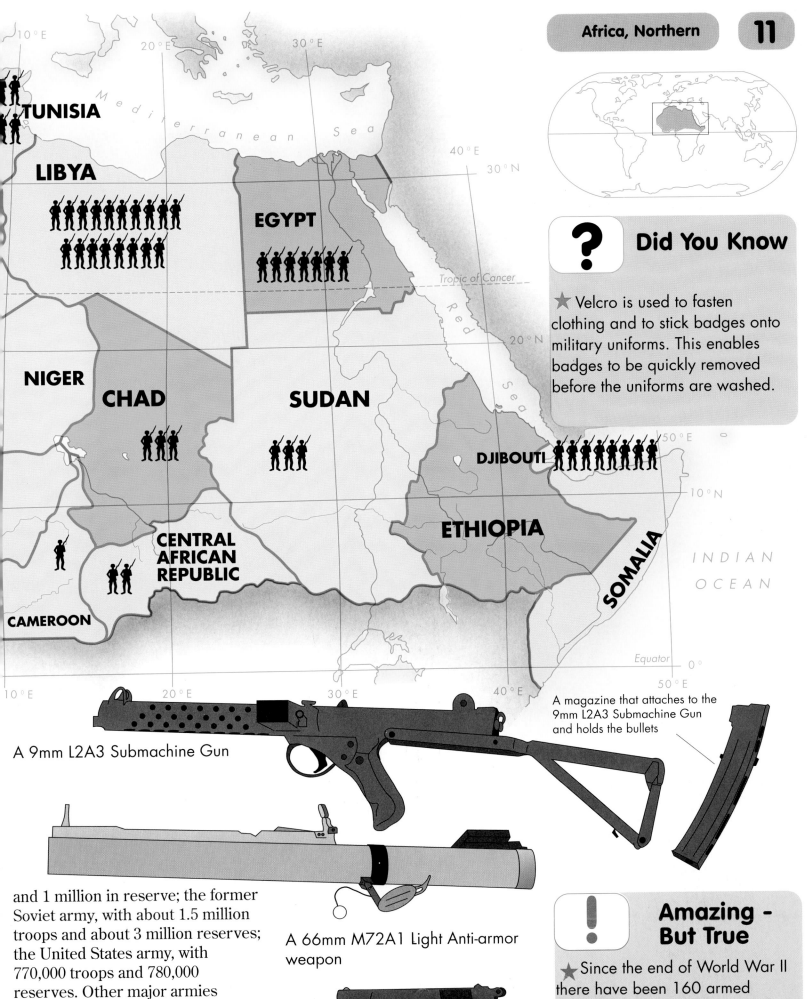

TUNISIA

LIBYA

EGYPT

NIGER

CHAD

SUDAN

DJIBOUTI

CENTRAL
AFRICAN
REPUBLIC

ETHIOPIA

SOMALIA

CAMEROON

*INDIAN
OCEAN*

Tropic of Cancer

Mediterranean Sea

Red Sea

Equator

? Did You Know

★ Velcro is used to fasten clothing and to stick badges onto military uniforms. This enables badges to be quickly removed before the uniforms are washed.

A magazine that attaches to the 9mm L2A3 Submachine Gun and holds the bullets

A 9mm L2A3 Submachine Gun

A 66mm M72A1 Light Anti-armor weapon

A 9mm Browning Pistol

and 1 million in reserve; the former Soviet army, with about 1.5 million troops and about 3 million reserves; the United States army, with 770,000 troops and 780,000 reserves. Other major armies are the German, French, British, Egyptian, Israeli, Indian, Iraqi, North Korean, Pakistani, South Korean, Turkish, and Vietnamese armies.

! Amazing - But True

★ Since the end of World War II there have been 160 armed conflicts — most of them in developing countries and none formally declared. Over half have been civil wars.

A number of long civil wars have raged on in southern Africa, but some encouraging progress has been made. In Angola a settlement to end the war has been agreed upon, and a fragile cease-fire operates in Mozambique. In South Africa, steps towards democracy are in progress, but civil unrest is increasing.

Civil Wars

Wars seem to be inevitable in human society, and the number that take place does not seem to be in decline. Although full-scale world war has been avoided since 1945, small wars have flourished and have been responsible for the deaths of more people than World War II.

Most of the motives have been political — such as attempts to overthrow a current government, — although many have had underlying social and economic causes.

One of the worst consequences of civil war is the number of refugees and displaced persons that result. In southern Africa alone, over 2 million people have been forced to leave their countries and homes. Many flee to neighboring countries, where they congregate in camps.

In Mozambique, where a rebel movement has caused destruction for over 10 years, about 800,000 Mozambicans have fled to Malawi, where they now place a huge burden on that nation's resources. The civil war in Angola also caused massive displacements of persons.

The victims of any war are the children who often become refugees. In parts of Africa this often results in thousands of starving homeless people.

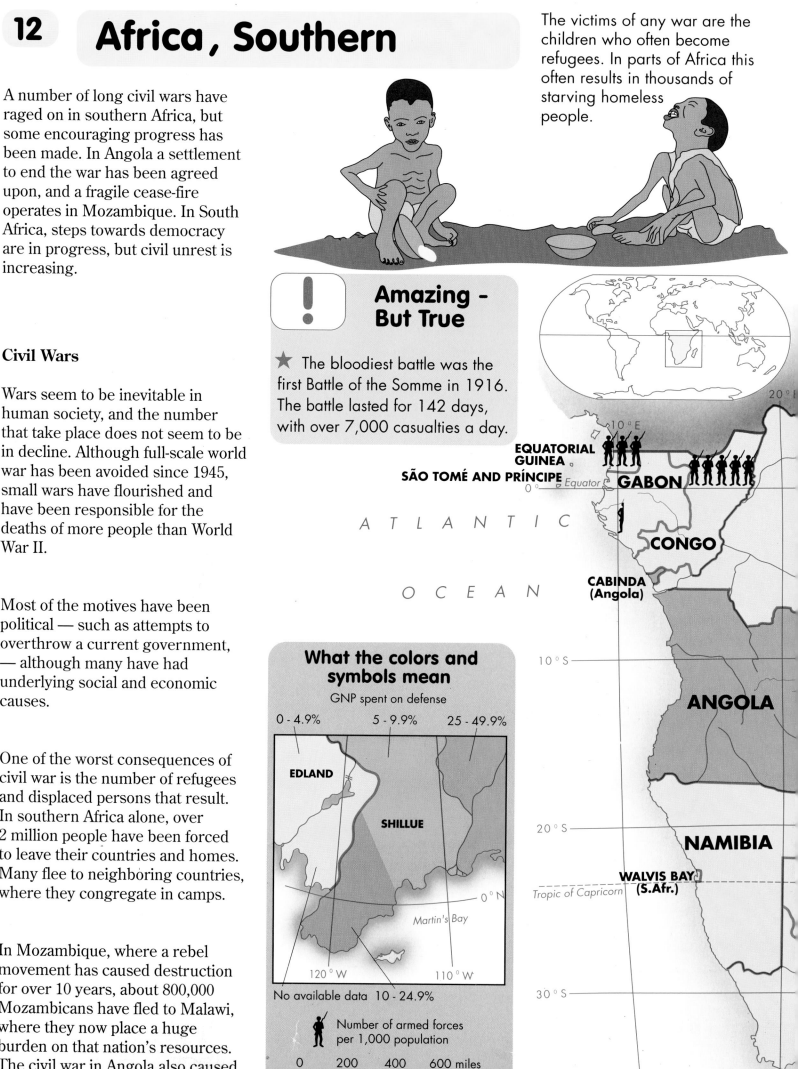

Amazing - But True

★ The bloodiest battle was the first Battle of the Somme in 1916. The battle lasted for 142 days, with over 7,000 casualties a day.

What the colors and symbols mean

GNP spent on defense

| 0 - 4.9% | 5 - 9.9% | 25 - 49.9% |

EDLAND

SHILLUE

0° N

Martin's Bay

120° W   110° W

No available data   10 - 24.9%

Number of armed forces per 1,000 population

0   200   400   600 miles

EQUATORIAL GUINEA
SÃO TOMÉ AND PRÍNCIPE   Equator   GABON
ATLANTIC
CONGO
CABINDA (Angola)
OCEAN
10° S
ANGOLA
20° S
NAMIBIA
WALVIS BAY (S.Afr.)
Tropic of Capricorn
30° S
10° E   20° E

Organization of African Unity

In 1963 the heads of 32 African countries signed a charter, the chief objects of which are the furtherance of African unity and solidarity and the coordination of political, cultural, health, scientific, and defense policies.

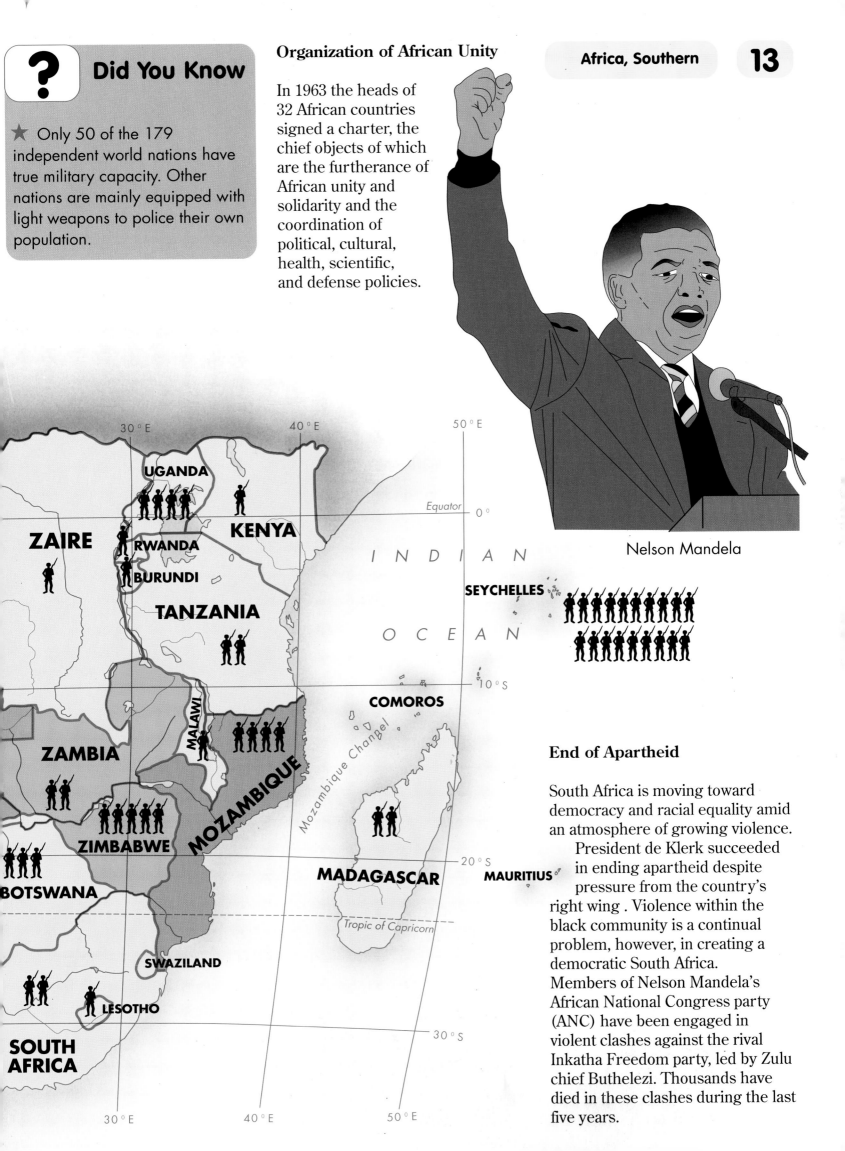

Nelson Mandela

End of Apartheid

South Africa is moving toward democracy and racial equality amid an atmosphere of growing violence. President de Klerk succeeded in ending apartheid despite pressure from the country's right wing . Violence within the black community is a continual problem, however, in creating a democratic South Africa. Members of Nelson Mandela's African National Congress party (ANC) have been engaged in violent clashes against the rival Inkatha Freedom party, led by Zulu chief Buthelezi. Thousands have died in these clashes during the last five years.

Civil war and guerrilla fighting have torn apart many of the small nations of Central America for many years. Guatemala, Honduras, Nicaragua, and El Salvador are all suffering from civil unrest. United States interest in this area is strong because of the importance of the Panama Canal.

Guerrilla War

Guerrilla war is waged by groups of people who want to overthrow their government. If people do not feel that the government is acting in their interests, and changes cannot be made by proper means, they may resort to these tactics.

The word *guerrilla* means "little war" in Spanish and was first used from 1808-14 in the Napoleonic Wars. This form of warfare is carried out by bands of fighters who torment the enemy with sudden ambushes and attacks, acts of sabotage, and unexpected raids. The fighters are usually grouped in small, well-organized bands and operate behind enemy lines using hit-and-run tactics. They are often called underground or resistance fighters, or partisans.

Guerrilla fighters often hide and ambush their targets.

Nationalist guerrillas object to a government controlled by another group. Revolutionary guerrillas try to overthrow the government, and counterrevolutionary guerrillas want to return to the previous political situation.

Guerrillas have been very successful at times. A famous guerrilla is the Cuban leader Fidel Castro, who began an attempt in 1953 to overthrow the country's government. He used strong appeals and propaganda along with guerrilla tactics. With his small band of revolutionaries, he became strong enough to take over the government in 1959.

★ During 1987 the world spent about $2 million a minute on defense.

★ There are over 50 military governments in the developing world.

★ U.S. forces are stationed in 360 bases in dozens of countries, Panama being one such country.

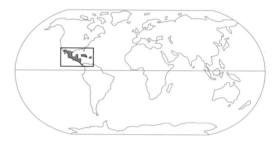

The Panama Canal

Panama is of strategic interest to the United States of America, as was made clear by its invasion of Panama in 1989. The Panama Canal will remain under the control of the United States until 1999.

The different sizes of warships

Frigate

Destroyer

Cruiser

Battleship

Aircraft carrier

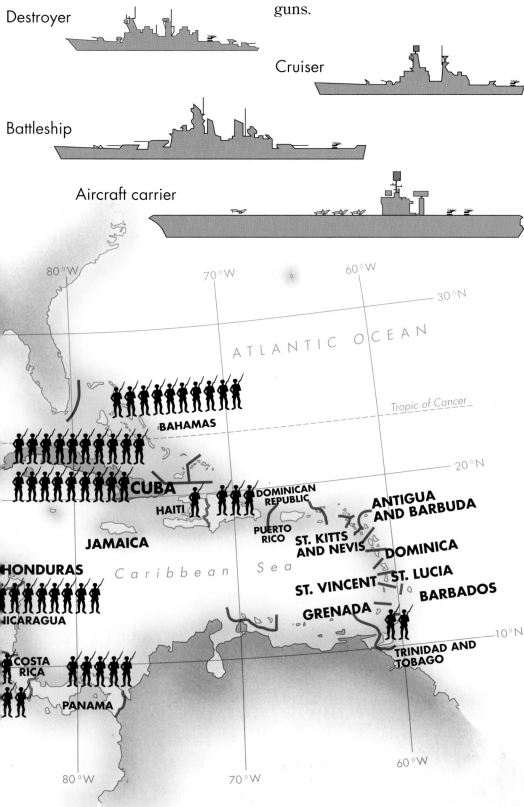

Carrier Warfare

Aircraft carriers were used in World War II, but afterward the cost and vulnerability of these huge vessels made them seem impractical. However, in the 1980s, they had a revival because they provided a seagoing base for military aircraft, thus enabling attacks on enemy aircraft to be carried out far beyond the range of a ship's own weapons. Aircraft carriers are equipped with fixed-wing aircraft, helicopters, missile launchers, and antiaircraft guns.

Cuba

The collapse of communism in Eastern Europe has left the socialist state of Cuba rather out on a limb. Fidel Castro still maintains his own brand of government and talks of "perfecting communism." A severe austerity program has been introduced to deal with the decline in the economy due to the loss of trade and subsidies from the former Soviet Union. Many urban workers have been sent back to the land because shortages of spare parts and fuel have made transport impossible. Horse-drawn carts and bicycles are replacing the motor car as this country moves backward. However, relations between Cuba and the United States, which have at times seemed close to war, may possibly improve.

Compartments of a ship

Machinery

Weapons

Accommodations

Control room

Auxilary machinery

Weapons

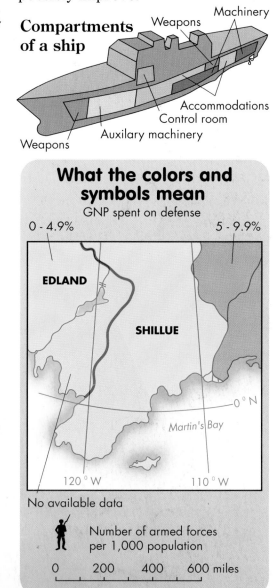

What the colors and symbols mean

GNP spent on defense

0 - 4.9%   5 - 9.9%

EDLAND

SHILLUE

Martin's Bay

No available data

Number of armed forces per 1,000 population

0   200   400   600 miles

The dispute between Great Britain and Argentina about the Falkland/Malvinas Islands has still not been resolved, despite a costly war in 1982. However, diplomatic relations between the countries have been restored. The production and sale of cocaine is a major issue between the United States and some South American nations.

Falklands War

In 1982, Argentina fought a bitter war with Great Britain over the Falkland Islands. Argentina had long laid claim to these islands, situated about 310 miles east of the Strait of Magellan. Since 1833 Britain had ruled the islands, which are called the Islas Malvinas by the Argentines.

In April 1982, Argentine troops moved in and reclaimed the islands. A fierce land, sea, and air battle was fought for control of the territory. A fleet of Royal Navy vessels, which consisted of carriers with vertical/short takeoff fighters, cruisers, destroyers, and nuclear-powered submarines, destroyed Argentine airpower and carried out a successful seaborne assault.

One of the most notable events of the war was the sinking of the Argentine cruiser *Belgrano* by the British nuclear attack submarine HMS *Conqueror,* which resulted in about 300 Argentine deaths. There were approximately 250 UK casualties in the war, and 1,500 Argentines lost their lives. The war cost £1.6 billion.

Argentina surrendered in June but has never abandoned its claim to the islands.

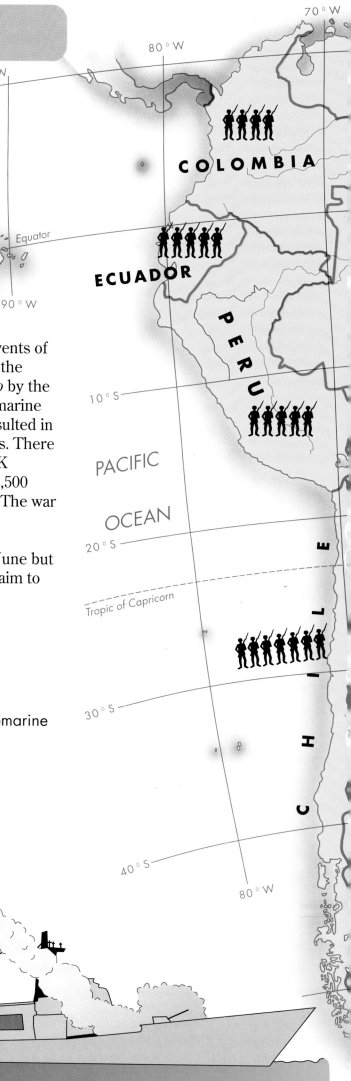

A Navy ship firing anti-submarine weapons.

? Did You Know

★ World War I saw the airplane and the tank being used for the first time.

★ Prior to the Falklands War, synthetic fibers were used for military uniforms, but these were highly inflammable. Now the trend is toward natural fibers such as cotton.

VENEZUELA

GUYANA
SURINAME
FRENCH GUIANA

60° W
10° N
50° W
40° W
Equator
0°

B R A Z I L

10° S

BOLIVIA

20° S

PARAGUAY

Tropic of Capricorn

ATLANTIC

OCEAN

30° S

40° W

Harrier

URUGUAY

A very successful fixed-wing aircraft, the Harrier is also called the jump jet. It is designed so that it can take off and land vertically in a very confined space with very little ground support, and it can refuel in midair.

50° W

UNITED STATES MARINES

50° S

Falkland Is. (U.K.)

Scotia Sea

70° W   60° W

The Hercules is the most widely used military transport plane in the world. Here you can see it in midflight refueling two Skyhawks.

Cocaine

One of the most heated issues between the United States and South America is the production and sale of cocaine. The United States government estimated that the sales of South American cocaine were valued at over $22 billion in 1987. Bolivia and Peru are the main producers, and Colombia is the center for refining and export. The Colombian government's attempts to destroy the drug cartels led to an all-out campaign of terror. Bolivia and Peru are trying to make payments and reimbursements to drug-growing peasants to stop the trade.

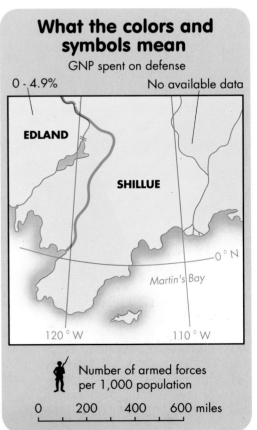

One of the horrors of the Falklands War was the sinking of ships and the loss of life.

What the colors and symbols mean

GNP spent on defense

0 - 4.9%   No available data

EDLAND

SHILLUE

0° N

Martin's Bay

120° W   110° W

🚶 Number of armed forces per 1,000 population

0   200   400   600 miles

An Antarctic treaty, signed in 1959 and lasting for 30 years, allows only peaceful scientific research to be conducted in this region. The main claims to the Antarctic are from Norway, Australia, France, New Zealand, Chile, Britain, and Argentina.

Military Uniforms

Uniforms are designed for the job in which they are needed and not just to keep soldiers looking the same. Here are some examples of the varying styles of uniform.

This Gurkha soldier is wearing a mottled green uniform to enable him to blend into the jungle and hide his movements from the enemy. The handle of his knife is covered with nonreflective tape, and the blade is covered with camouflage material.

SOUTHERN OCEAN

Scotia Sea

Drake Passage

Antarctic Circle

Weddell Sea

Bellingshausen Sea

Ross Sea

45°W 55°S 50°S 60°W 75 15°W 30°W 60°S 65°S 70°S 75°S 80°S 85°S 90°W 105°W 120°W 135°W 150°W 165°W

This naval antiaircraft gunner is wearing blue overalls, a yellow vest with his job title on the back to aid identification, and a life preserver. The Anti-Flash hood and gloves protect the flesh from burns and are worn by everyone on board a ship in action. The ear protectors are essential, as the noise of the gun is deafening.

A different kind of camouflage is the white suit worn during operations in snowy conditions. Even the gun and bags have a camouflage pattern to them, making the solider hard to see from the air or the ground. The use of skis enables the soldier to move quickly in difficult conditions.

This army uniform is for everyday use, and only the addition of badges differentiates the officer from the enlisted ranks. The length of the skirt changes with fashion.

This chemical suit is worn for protection, but it is uncomfortable to wear. It is designed to cover and seal the whole body from chemicals. In the oxygen mask there is a voice transmitter to make verbal communication possible.

This pilot's helmet has a specially modified visor to increase his upward visibilty and is worn with the oxygen mask. The parachute is part of the ejector seat, and the pilot has a special harness and gravity suit that also attaches to the seat. He carries a life preserver, which would inflate if he landed in water.

China, one of the strongest military powers in the world, seems to be improving its relationship with its neighbor Russia. Arms exports from China are still a major concern for many countries.

The Nuclear Arms Race

Scientists had gained an understanding of the basic structure of the atom by the early 20th century, and in 1938 researchers discovered that by splitting the nucleus of a uranium atom a great deal of energy could be released. By the beginning of World War II U.S. physicists were aware of the military applications of nuclear energy. They were very concerned that Nazi Germany might develop a nuclear weapon. In August 1939 Albert Einstein, a German-born physicist, made the president of the United States aware of the potential military applications of nuclear energy.

? Did You Know

★ The atomic bomb dropped on the Japanese city of Hiroshima destroyed four square miles of the city and killed more than 70,000 people.

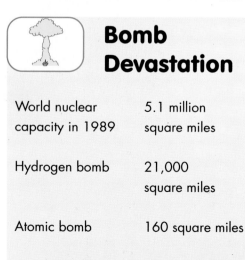

Bomb Devastation

World nuclear capacity in 1989	5.1 million square miles
Hydrogen bomb	21,000 square miles
Atomic bomb	160 square miles
Hiroshima destroyed	4 square miles

The effects of a nuclear explosion

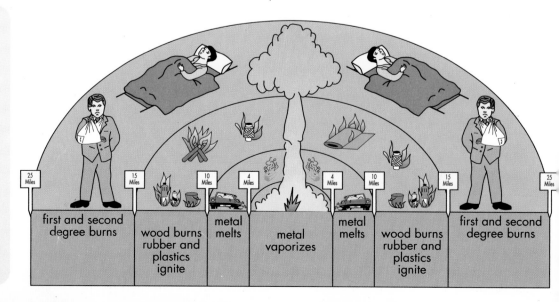

| first and second degree burns | wood burns rubber and plastics ignite | metal melts | metal vaporizes | metal melts | wood burns rubber and plastics ignite | first and second degree burns |

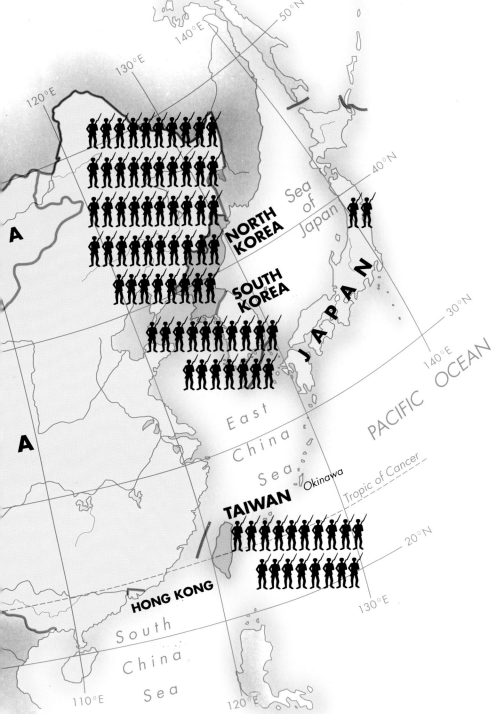

the United States in the 1970s, followed closely by the Soviet Union. By the late 1970s a type of weapon known as a neutron bomb, which would kill soldiers on battlefields but do less damage to civilians and buildings, had been developed by scientists in the United States. By the mid-1980s the emphasis had changed to developing a new type of device called a third-generation nuclear weapon — for use in a system of defense against nuclear attack.

During the cold war arms race, protests against nuclear weapons were mounted in some Western countries.

Today many people believe the political developments of the late 1980s and early 1990s have marked the end of the cold war. In Europe, there is much less concern about the possibility of a massive conventional attack. It is expected that nuclear military arsenals will gradually be reduced.

The U.S. government set up the Manhattan Project to design and build a nuclear bomb. The first experimental device was exploded in 1945 by J. Robert Oppenheimer. The first weapon was used by the United States against Japan. It was dropped from an aircraft on Hiroshima on August 6, 1945. Three days later another bomb was dropped on Nagasaki.

Tension developed between the Soviet Union and the United States in the late 1940s, resulting in the so-called cold war. The nuclear arms race was an important feature of the cold war, for as mutual suspicions grew between the two

main powers, they both invested huge amounts of money and research into developing weapons. In 1949 the Soviet Union tested its first fusion device. In 1952 the United States exploded its first thermonuclear device. In the mid-1950s the Soviets built the first nuclear-equipped submarines. In 1957 they test-launched their first land-based intercontinental ballistic missile (ICBM). The first U.S. ICBM became operational in 1959. Also in 1959 the U.S.A. commissioned its first nuclear submarines.

The first MIRVs (missiles with multiple warheads) were made by

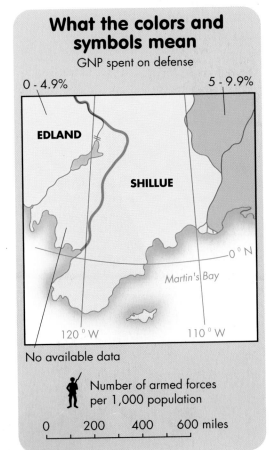

What the colors and symbols mean

GNP spent on defense

0 - 4.9%   5 - 9.9%

No available data

Number of armed forces per 1,000 population

0   200   400   600 miles

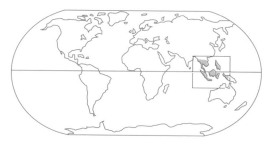

Military strength is an important factor in the governments of many Southeast Asian countries. Civil wars and Communist uprisings are only recent history in many places. Indonesia, for instance, suffered huge losses in human terms during its Communist uprising.

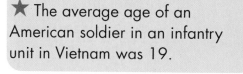

Amazing - But True

★ The average age of an American soldier in an infantry unit in Vietnam was 19.

The Vietnam War

The Vietnam War began in 1957. At first the U.S. Army only contributed advisers, but as its commitment grew units were sent into action. At its peak in 1969, U.S. Army strength in Vietnam was 365,000.

Fighting was very heavy, and the airmobile divisions proved very effective. Helicopters were a major weapon and were used as armed attack vehicles, troop and cargo carriers, and mobile ambulances.

A cease-fire was signed in 1973, and afterward the U.S. government ended its military draft. Now the armed forces are all volunteers. The war ended finally in 1975.

The Chinook has two large rotors that turn in opposite directions so that the helicopter does not spin.

A Lynx helicopter is used for naval warfare and on the battlefield.

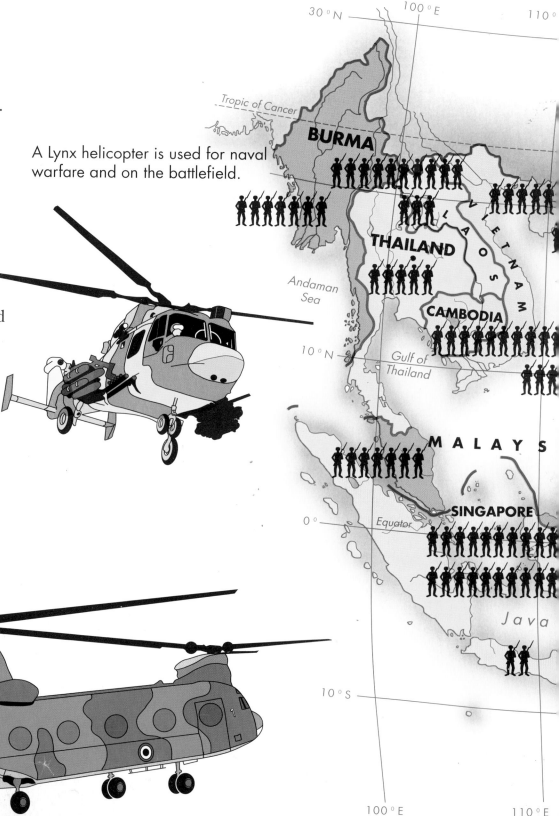

Association of Southeast Asian Nations (ASEAN)

Formed in August 1967, its main objectives are to accelerate economic growth, social progress, and cultural developments; promote active collaboration and mutual assistance in matters of common interest; and to ensure the stability of the Southeast Asia region.

Members: Indonesia, Malaysia, Philippines, Singapore, Thailand, and Brunei.

? Did You Know

⭐ Between 1945 and 1975, the war in Vietnam cost the lives of at least 2 million Vietnamese, 74,000 French, and 58,000 Americans.

⭐ Between 1969 and 1971, drug use among U.S. forces rose by 20% due to poor morale.

⭐ By 1971 nearly 5.5 million acres of South Vietnamese forest and cropland had been sprayed with chemicals by the U.S.A. to strip trees of their foliage. This enabled enemy movements to be plotted more easily.

Geneva Convention

The first Geneva Convention was signed in 1864 and accepted by all European countries and the United States, some countries in Asia, and some in South America. It provided for the humane treatment of civilians, prisoners, and wounded persons in wartime.

Methods are provided to identify the dead and wounded and send information to their families. The protection of hospitals and medical transport and their proper marking with a red cross are also specified.

During the Vietnam War, when fighting grew very heavy, each side accused the other of transgressing the accepted rules of conducting warfare as set out by the Geneva Convention. In 1969 it was determined that U.S. troops had massacred hundreds of civilians in the area around My Lai. As a result, the U.S. Army court-martialed several officers and enlisted men for war crimes.

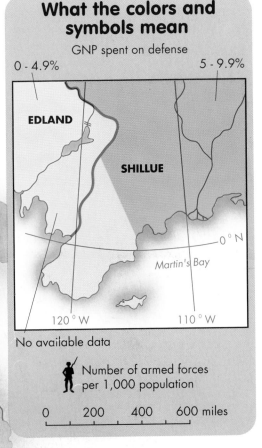

What the colors and symbols mean

GNP spent on defense

0 - 4.9%   5 - 9.9%

EDLAND

SHILLUE

Martin's Bay

No available data

👤 Number of armed forces per 1,000 population

0   200   400   600 miles

Modern and well-equipped armed forces are part of the defense strategy of Australia and New Zealand, with a tradition of fierce fighting forces based on participation in two world wars.

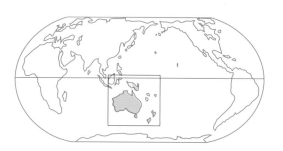

Types of Nuclear Weapons

The first nuclear weapons were fission bombs used in World War II (1939-1945) on the Japanese cities of Hiroshima and Nagasaki. This forced Japan to end the war. The Hiroshima bomb caused the worst destruction, killing 70,000 to 100,000 people and destroyed about four square miles. Most of today's large thermonuclear weapons are 8 to 40 times more powerful than the Hiroshima bomb.

Theater nuclear weapons are designed to be used in conventional warfare. Tactical nuclear weapons, as they are generally known, include medium-range ballistic missiles and cruise missiles, artillery shells, nuclear mines, and torpedoes.

SS-N-20 is the largest former Soviet ballistic missile at 49 feet long.

Trident D-5 is the largest US and UK ballistic missile at 44 feet long.

These missiles are relative in size to the submarines shown here.

? Did You Know

★ Australia refuses entry to its ports for warships confirmed to be carrying nuclear warheads.

★ New Zealand does not allow nuclear weapons on its territory and has none of its own.

Strategic and Theater Nuclear Weapons

These are the two main types of nuclear weapons that exist today. Strategic nuclear weapons are designed to launch an attack from a great distance on targets in the enemy's own territory. Weapons are delivered on long-range bomber aircraft or by missiles. These can travel up to 6,500 miles from their launch site.

Some of the missile launch sites are on land, but other missiles are launched underwater from submarines. These missiles are known as intercontinental ballistic missiles (ICBMs), submarine-launched ballistic missiles (SLBMs) or cruise missiles. Some strategic nuclear weapons have a number of warheads that can each be separately targeted. These are known as Multiple Independently Targetable Re-entry Vehicles (MIRVs).

What the colors and symbols mean

GNP spent on defense

0 - 4.9%

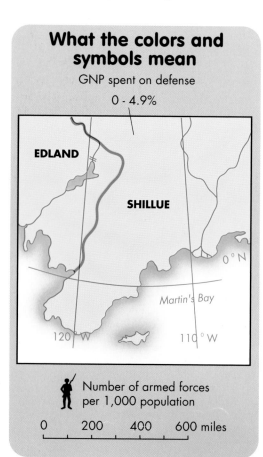

EDLAND

SHILLUE

0° N

Martin's Bay

120° W   110° W

Number of armed forces per 1,000 population

0   200   400   600 miles

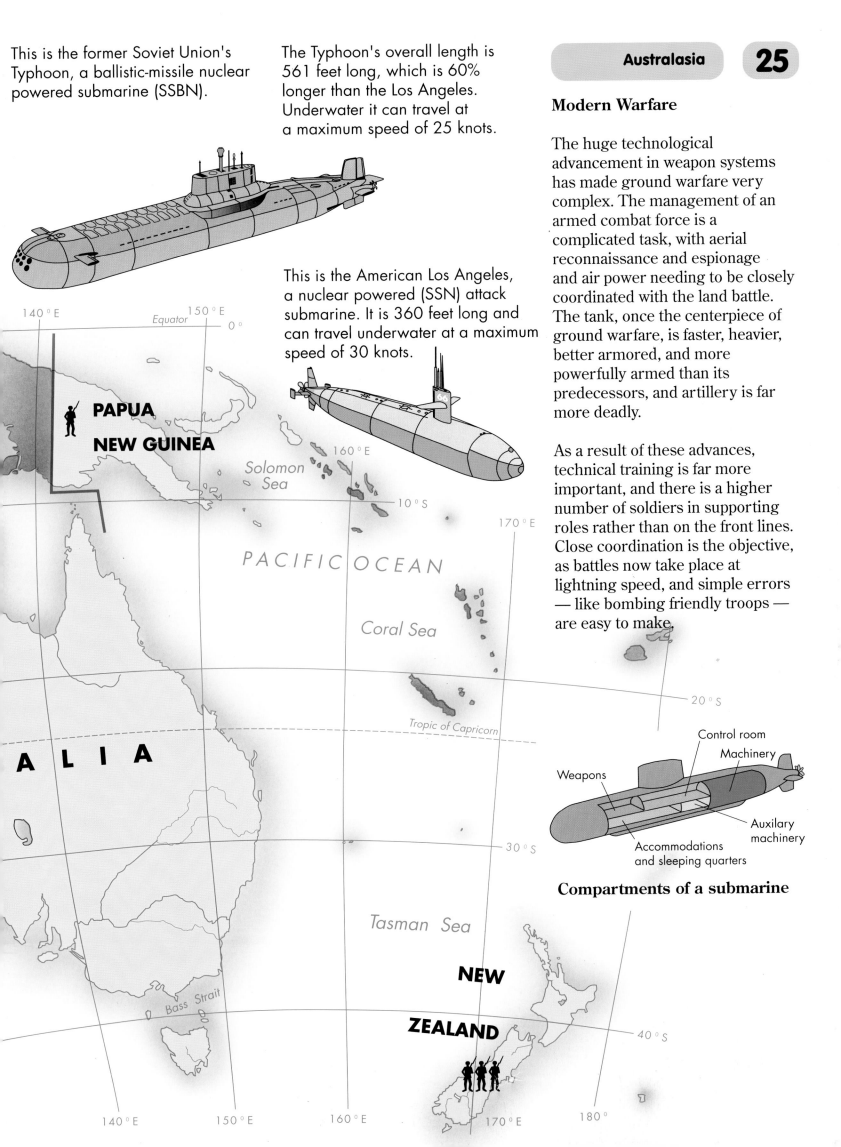

This is the former Soviet Union's Typhoon, a ballistic-missile nuclear powered submarine (SSBN).

The Typhoon's overall length is 561 feet long, which is 60% longer than the Los Angeles. Underwater it can travel at a maximum speed of 25 knots.

This is the American Los Angeles, a nuclear powered (SSN) attack submarine. It is 360 feet long and can travel underwater at a maximum speed of 30 knots.

Modern Warfare

The huge technological advancement in weapon systems has made ground warfare very complex. The management of an armed combat force is a complicated task, with aerial reconnaissance and espionage and air power needing to be closely coordinated with the land battle. The tank, once the centerpiece of ground warfare, is faster, heavier, better armored, and more powerfully armed than its predecessors, and artillery is far more deadly.

As a result of these advances, technical training is far more important, and there is a higher number of soldiers in supporting roles rather than on the front lines. Close coordination is the objective, as battles now take place at lightning speed, and simple errors — like bombing friendly troops — are easy to make.

PAPUA NEW GUINEA

Solomon Sea

PACIFIC OCEAN

Coral Sea

Tropic of Capricorn

A L I A

Tasman Sea

NEW ZEALAND

Bass Strait

140°E 150°E *Equator* 0° 160°E 10°S 170°E 20°S 30°S 40°S 180° 140°E 150°E 160°E 170°E

Control room
Machinery
Weapons
Auxilary machinery
Accommodations and sleeping quarters

Compartments of a submarine

Canada has a well-equipped national defense force organized to protect national interests at home and abroad, defend North America from attack, and carry out duties as a member of NATO.

North Atlantic Treaty Organization (NATO)

NATO provides a unified military leadership for 16 Western countries. It was established in 1950 as a collective defense against the Soviet Union. The basis of the treaty is that an armed attack against one of the member nations would be considered an attack against all. In 1990 Germany was reunified and replaced West Germany as a member nation.

To deter an attack by an aggressor, NATO relies partly on nuclear weapons, and the U.S.A. provides most of these. The dependence on U.S. nuclear weapons has made the U.S.A. a dominant member of NATO.

During the mid-1980s, NATO perceived a growing Soviet threat, and this led to the installation of more U.S. nuclear missiles in Britain and other NATO nations. Soviet leader Mikhail Gorbachev soon began to seek better relations with the U.S.A. and the other NATO countries, and tensions began to decline.

In 1988 the United States and the Soviet Union signed a treaty to eliminate the ground-launched, medium-range missiles of both countries. By the late 1980s the Soviet Union had, in addition, begun to cut its conventional forces stationed in Eastern Europe. Gorbachev began to allow increased democracy in the Soviet Union and to encourage similar movements in Eastern Europe.

As a result non-Communist parties came into power.

In 1990 the NATO countries and the Soviet Union and its eastern allies signed agreements prohibiting the use of military force against each other. They also agreed to destroy large numbers of their tanks, artillery, and non-nuclear weapons in Europe.

The structure of NATO

The members of NATO's Council

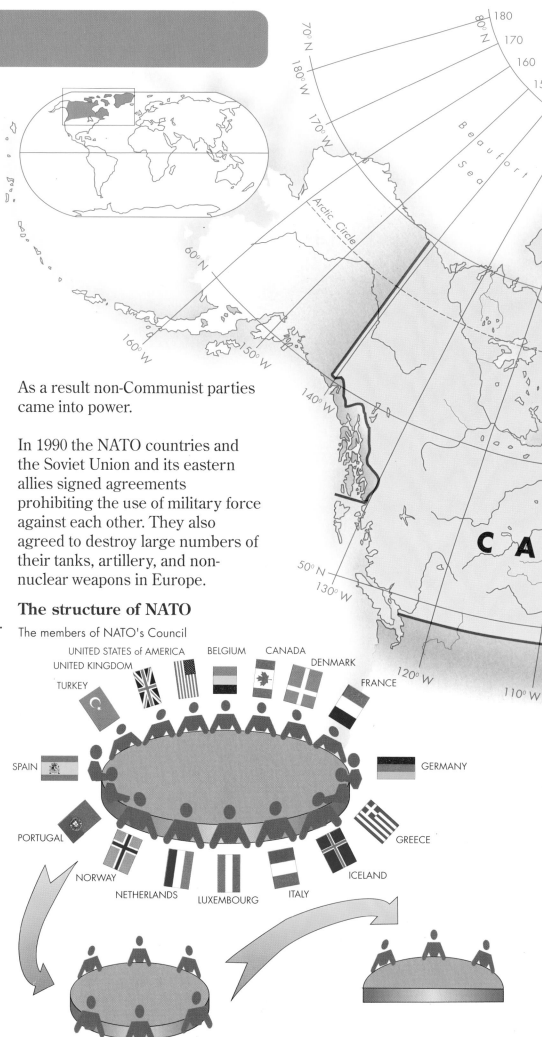

Military Committee made up of national chiefs of staff who meet twice a year.

The SACEUR, Supreme Allied Commander of Europe, of which there are three.

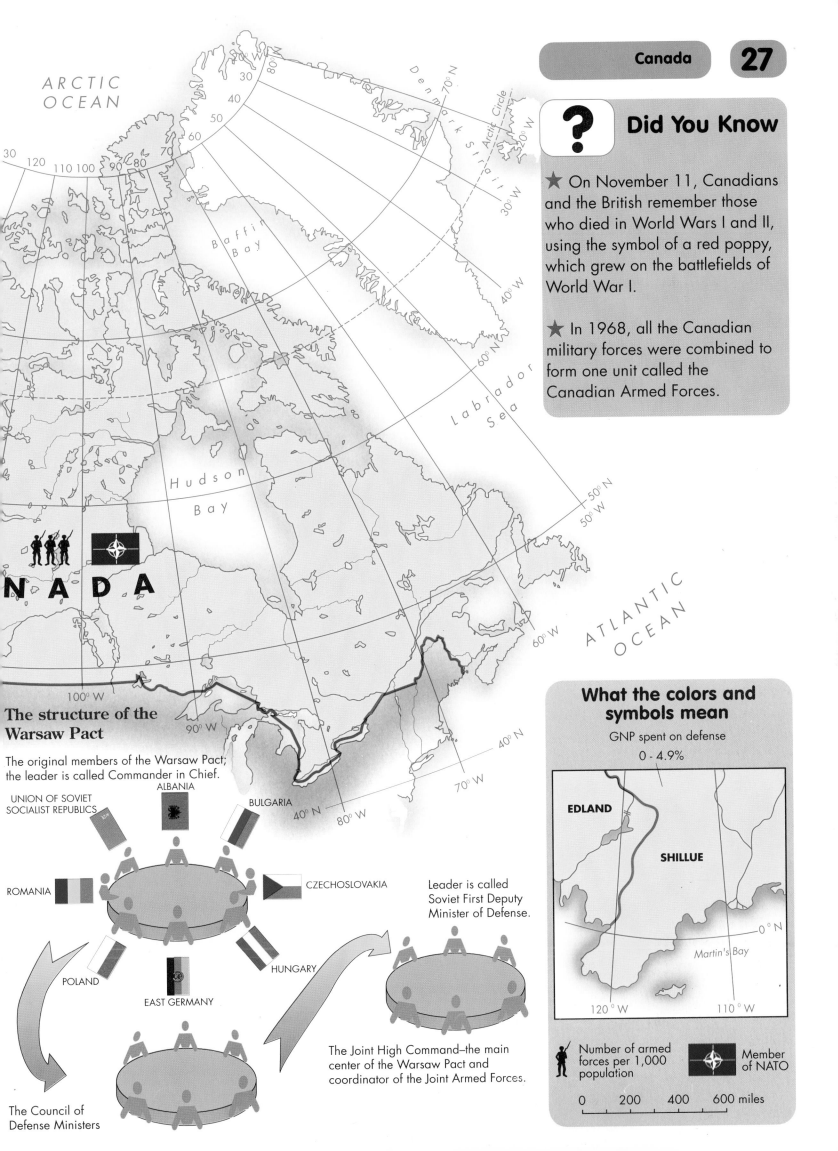

ARCTIC
OCEAN

Baffin Bay

Denmark Strait

Arctic Circle

Hudson Bay

Labrador Sea

N A D A

ATLANTIC OCEAN

? Did You Know

★ On November 11, Canadians and the British remember those who died in World Wars I and II, using the symbol of a red poppy, which grew on the battlefields of World War I.

★ In 1968, all the Canadian military forces were combined to form one unit called the Canadian Armed Forces.

The structure of the Warsaw Pact

The original members of the Warsaw Pact; the leader is called Commander in Chief.

UNION OF SOVIET SOCIALIST REPUBLICS

ALBANIA

BULGARIA

ROMANIA

CZECHOSLOVAKIA

POLAND

EAST GERMANY

HUNGARY

Leader is called Soviet First Deputy Minister of Defense.

The Joint High Command–the main center of the Warsaw Pact and coordinator of the Joint Armed Forces.

The Council of Defense Ministers

What the colors and symbols mean

GNP spent on defense
0 - 4.9%

EDLAND

SHILLUE

Martin's Bay

Number of armed forces per 1,000 population

Member of NATO

| 0 | 200 | 400 | 600 miles |

Until recently, the CIS was the strongest military power in terms of manpower. The breakup of the Union of Soviet Socialist Republics has led to a great deal of anxiety about the control of the powerful nuclear weapons developed during the period of the cold war.

Control of Nuclear Weapons

Because of the immense danger of nuclear weapons, many attempts have been made to control them. The chief means have been strategies of deterrence and placing limits on their testing, number, and proliferation.

Deterrence

The theory of deterrence states that the possession of a strong nuclear force by two opposing countries will prevent a war between them. The theory relies on the aggressor believing that the other side holds a force large enough to return an attack that would cause unacceptable destruction.

Limiting Numbers

Attempts to control the number of nuclear weapons in the world began in 1970. Limits were first established between the United States and the former Soviet Union in their Strategic Arms Limitation Talks (SALT).

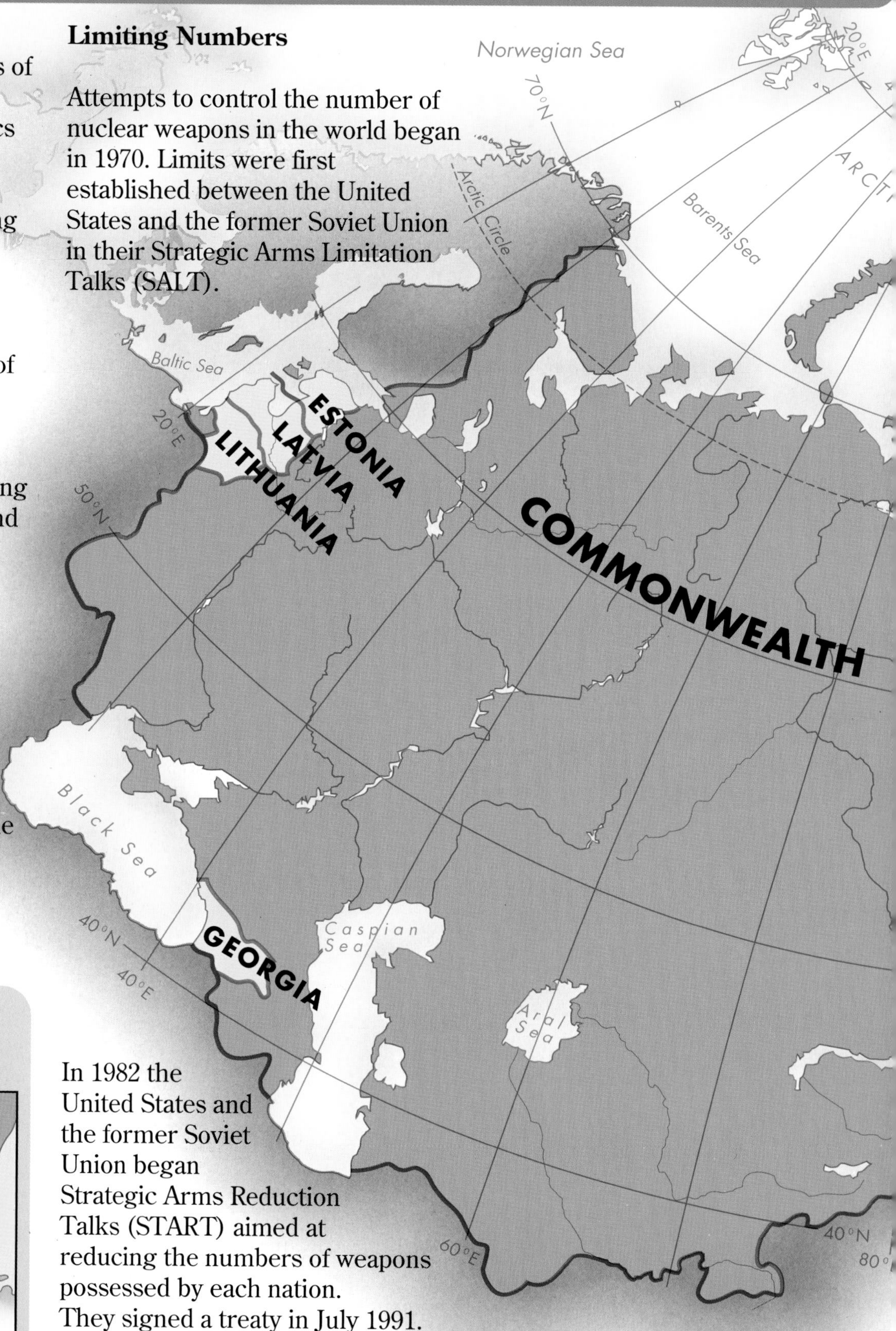

In 1982 the United States and the former Soviet Union began Strategic Arms Reduction Talks (START) aimed at reducing the numbers of weapons possessed by each nation. They signed a treaty in July 1991.

Nonproliferation

This aims to prevent the spread of nuclear weapons to other nations that do not already have them. A treaty on the Nonproliferation of Nuclear Weapons was approved by the United Nations in 1968 and has been ratified by 130 countries.

What the colors and symbols mean

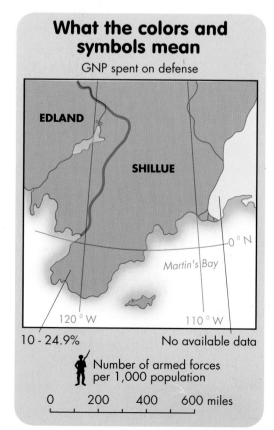

GNP spent on defense

EDLAND

SHILLUE

Martin's Bay

120°W   110°W

10 - 24.9%   No available data

Number of armed forces per 1,000 population

0   200   400   600 miles

Amazing – But True

★ The USA and CIS together spend more money on defense than the rest of the world.

Map labels: Norwegian Sea, Barents Sea, Arctic Circle, Baltic Sea, ESTONIA, LATVIA, LITHUANIA, COMMONWEALTH, Black Sea, GEORGIA, Caspian Sea, Aral Sea, 70°N, 20°E, 50°N, 40°N, 40°E, 60°E, 80°

OF INDEPENDENT STATES

East Siberian Sea

Arctic Circle

70°N

60°N

180

Bering Sea

50°N

Sea of Okhotsk

PACIFIC OCEAN

160°E

40°N

120°E

100°E

140°E

40°N

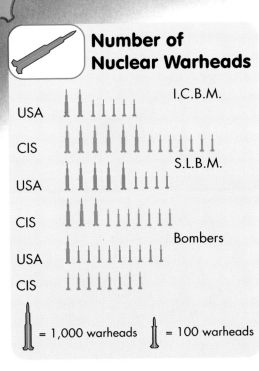

Number of Nuclear Warheads

	I.C.B.M.
USA	
CIS	
	S.L.B.M.
USA	
CIS	
	Bombers
USA	
CIS	

= 1,000 warheads   = 100 warheads

Disarmament — Arms Control

Limiting, reducing, or regulating a nation's armed forces and weapons is known as arms control, or disarmament.

The power of modern weapons exceeds any real purpose. Today a nuclear submarine can carry missiles and nuclear warheads that contain more destructive power than all the weapons used during World War II.

A nuclear war might produce dust and debris to change the earth's climate. Many scientists believe such a war could threaten every part of the world.

The threat of the use of nuclear weapons against a country might cause a war. A threatened country fearing its own survival might attack first.

Arms control aims to reduce the need for countries to acquire nuclear weapons or increase their supply.

Quiet for many years, in the 1980s eastern Europe erupted to overthrow Communist governments. The Warsaw Pact was abandoned in 1991, and the withdrawal of Soviet forces has taken place. However, ethnic tensions that have been repressed have spilled out in some bitter civil wars, particularly in what was previously Yugoslavia.

Warsaw Pact

The Warsaw Pact was the treaty that bound most of the Eastern European nations in a military command under Soviet control. It was signed by Albania, Bulgaria, Czechoslovakia, East Germany, Hungary, Poland, Romania, and the Soviet Union in May 1955. Albania withdrew in 1968. These countries claimed that they joined forces as a response to the creation of NATO in 1950.

Soviet control declined in 1989 and 1990 as a result of Communist parties being driven from power in Poland, Hungary, East Germany, and Czechoslovakia by means of peaceful revolutions. Hungary declared it would no longer participate in military operations and withdrew in 1991. Poland and Czechoslovakia announced plans to withdraw, and East Germany's membership ended in 1990 when it became part of a united Germany. Thus the Warsaw Pact's effectiveness as a military alliance ended.

Arms Spending

In 1989 it was estimated that the world's arms spending was running at an annual rate of $110 trillion or 5.4% of world GNP. In 1987 there were 28,123,000 full-time armed forces regulars or conscripts and 40,289,400 reservists in the world.

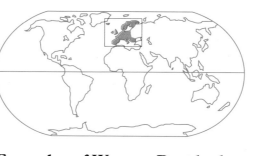

Examples of Warsaw Pact badges

Vehicle Insignia   Sleeve Insignia

Czechoslovak Army

Hungarian Army

Polish Army

! Amazing - But True

★ When Alfred Nobel, the Swedish engineer, invented the explosive dynamite, he thought it was a weapon so terrible that wars would no longer be fought.

★ The first aerial bombs were dropped from balloons on Venice by the Austrians in 1849.

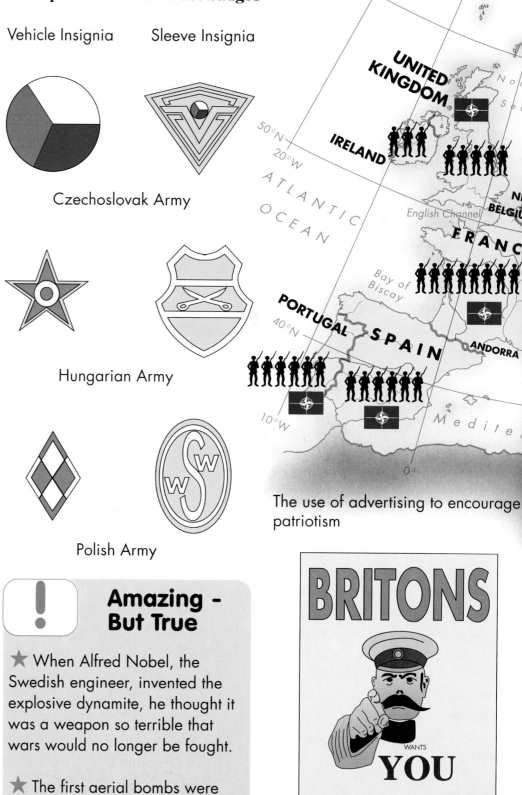

The use of advertising to encourage patriotism

BRITONS

WANTS

YOU

JOIN YOUR COUNTRY'S ARMY!
GOD SAVE THE KING

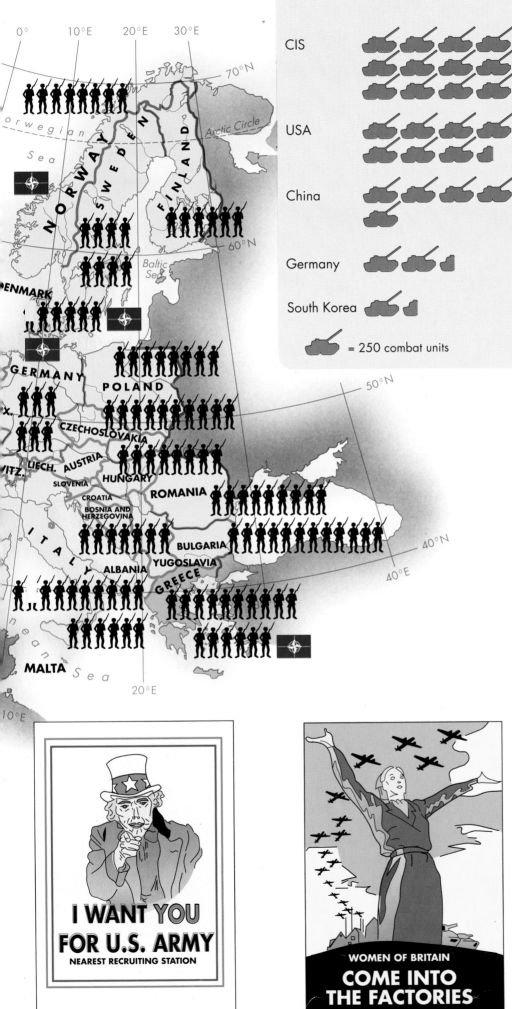

Most Combat Units

CIS	(tanks)
USA	(tanks)
China	(tanks)
Germany	(tanks)
South Korea	(tanks)

= 250 combat units

Yugoslavia

By the end of 1991 the old Yugoslavia had ceased to exist. Slovenia declared independence and Croatia followed suit, but not without a bloody civil war with heavy destruction and loss of life. Both Bosnia-Herzegovina and Macedonia voted for independence in 1992, but ethnic and border complications abound. There are Serb, Croat, and Muslim minorities in Bosnia-Herzegovina, while Macedonia claims part of northern Greece. Only Bosnia-Herzegovina has obtained independence so far.

? Did You Know

★ The first tank was driven into battle by the British in 1916.

★ During World War II, the Germans developed a pilotless aircraft with explosives in its nose — 'flying bombs.'

What the colors and symbols mean

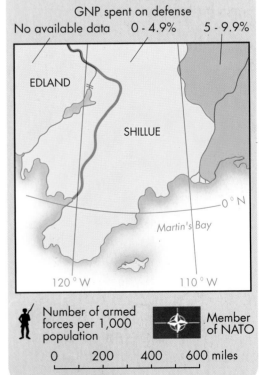

GNP spent on defense

No available data   0 - 4.9%   5 - 9.9%

EDLAND

SHILLUE

0° N

Martin's Bay

120° W   110° W

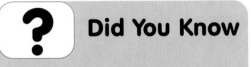
Number of armed forces per 1,000 population

Member of NATO

0   200   400   600 miles

I WANT YOU FOR U.S. ARMY
NEAREST RECRUITING STATION

WOMEN OF BRITAIN COME INTO THE FACTORIES

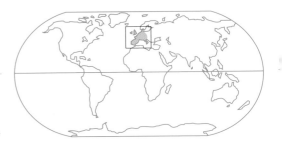

The excitement over the end of the long cold war has not yet resulted in a military reorganization in Western Europe. Most NATO members are intent on reviewing their military forces and making reductions.

United Nations

The United Nations was created to prevent international conflicts. Its work in this area has often been undervalued. UN peacekeeping forces have performed their role in many of the world's trouble spots, and without their presence there would almost certainly have been more bloodshed.

Peacekeeping forces at present in operation:

1. United Nations Truce Supervision Organization (UNTSO).
Established in 1948 to assist in supervising the truce in Palestine. Strength 300 (stationed in Beirut, South Lebanon, Sinai, Jordan, Israel, Syria).

2. United Nations Military Observer Group in India and Pakistan (UNMOGIP).
To supervise the cease-fire between India and Pakistan along the Line of Control. Strength 35 (stationed in the state of Jammu and Kashmir).

3. United Nations Iran-Iraq Military Observer Group (UNIIMOG).
Established in 1988 to monitor the compliance of both sides with the cease-fire and supervise withdrawal of troops. Expired February 1991.

4. United Nations Angola Verification Mission (UNAVEM).
To verify the withdrawl of Cuban troops from Angola. Completed May 1991.

5. United Nations Angola Verification Mission II (UNAVEM II).Established June 1991 to verify the cease-fire between Angola and UNITA. Strength 350 military and 90 police observers.

6. United Nations Observer Group in Central America (ONUCA).
For verification of the Guatemala Agreement of 1987, including the ending of aid to irregular forces and use of territory of a state for attacking others. In 1990 the agreement was expanded to include taking delivery of and destroying arms and ammunition of the Nicaraguan Resistance as they demobilized. Strength 1,100 (stationed in El Salvador, Honduras, and Nicaragua).

7. United Nations Peacekeeping Force in Cyprus (UNFICYP).
Established in 1964 to prevent the recurrence of fighting and to contribute to the maintenance and restoration of law and order. Since the hostilities of 1974 it has supervised the cease-fire and maintained a buffer between the lines of the Cyprus National Guard and the Turkish-Cypriot forces. Strength 2,200.

8. United Nations Disengagement Observer Force (UNDOF).
To supervise the cease-fire between Israel and Syria, establish an area of separation, and verify troop levels as set out in the Agreement of Disengagement of 1974. Strength 1,300.

9. United Nations Interim Force in Lebanon (UNIFIL).
Established in 1978 to confirm the withdrawal of Israeli forces from southern Lebanon and restore international peace and security. Strength 5,900.

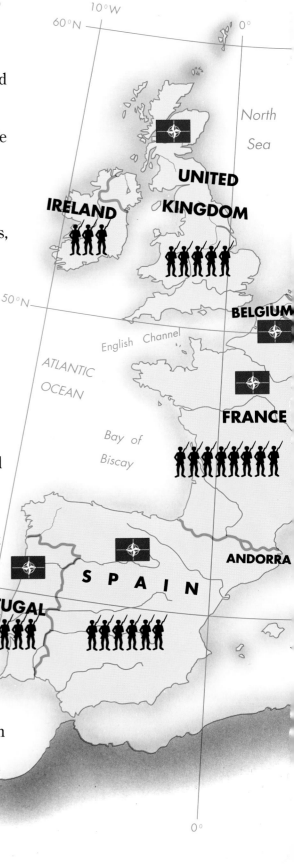

Did You Know

★ World War II cost Britain £34,423 million, which was 5 times more expensive than World War I.

★ The largest military retreat in history was from Dunkirk, France, in May, 1940, when over 338,000 British and French troops were evacuated.

✝ World War II Dead

Soviet Union	✝✝✝✝✝✝✝✝✝✝ ✝✝✝✝✝✝✝✝
China	✝✝✝✝ ✝✝✝✝
Japan	✝✝ ✝✝✝✝✝✝✝✝
United States	✝✝✝✝✝✝✝✝✝✝
Austria	✝✝✝✝✝✝✝ ✝✝✝✝✝
Great Britain	✝✝✝✝✝✝ ✝✝✝✝✝✝
Poland	✝✝✝✝✝✝✝ ✝✝✝✝
Romania	✝✝✝✝✝✝✝
France	✝✝✝✝✝✝
Hungary	✝✝✝✝✝✝✝✝✝

Casualties

✝ = 500,000   ✝ = 50,000   ✝ = 5,000

✝ World War I Casualties

Germany	✝✝✝✝✝✝✝✝
Russia	✝✝✝✝✝✝✝✝✝✝ ✝✝✝✝
France	✝✝✝✝✝✝✝✝✝✝ ✝✝✝✝
Austria - Hungary	✝✝✝✝✝✝✝ ✝✝✝✝✝✝✝
British Empire	✝✝✝✝✝✝✝✝✝✝ ✝✝
Italy	✝✝✝✝✝✝✝✝✝
Romania	✝✝✝✝✝✝✝✝✝✝✝
Ottoman Empire	✝✝✝✝✝✝✝✝
Bulgaria	✝✝✝✝✝✝✝✝

Casualties

✝ = 500,000   ✝ = 50,000   ✝ = 5,000

10. Office of the Secretary General in Afghanistan and Pakistan (OSGAP).
To assist in the implementation of the General Assembly Resolution of 1989. Strength 10.

11. United Nations Iraq/Kuwait Observer Mission (UNIKOM). Established in April 1991 following the recapture of Kuwait from Iraq. Its mission is to deter violations of the boundary and to observe hostile or potentially hostile actions.

12. United Nations Mission for the Referendum in Western Sahara (MINURSO). Established in April 1991.

What the colors and symbols mean

GNP spent on defense 0 - 4.9%

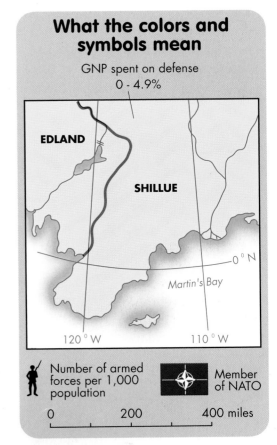

🚶 Number of armed forces per 1,000 population

✶ Member of NATO

0   200   400 miles

India and Pakistan both have very strong military forces with the capability to use nuclear weapons. Military tension exists between these two powerful countries. Meanwhile, fighting continues in Afghanistan between the government and the Mujaheddin.

Terrorism

Terrorists employ systematic violence and intimidation to achieve their political aims. The purpose of the violence is to create fear and alarm. Some of the tactics used include hijacking airplanes, setting off bombs, kidnapping, murder, and setting fire to buildings. Terrorists usually attack people who oppose their cause or people and objects that symbolize opposition. Kidnapping and murder victims include journalists, political leaders, businessmen, police, judges, and diplomats. Targets include oil refineries, government offices, and public buildings.

There is nothing new about terrorism. Tactics such as these were used by the American Ku Klux Klan to frighten blacks and their sympathizers in the early 1900s. The Provisional IRA in Northern Ireland uses violence to try and rid the country of British rule.

In the 1980s terrorists from groups in the Middle East posed a very real threat to governments. During the period 1980–86 there were 83 airplanes hijacked on domestic and international flights throughout the world. Aircraft provided vulnerable targets on which a solitary saboteur could prove very destructive. Governments and airlines have worked hard to tighten security in a bid to counter this threat.

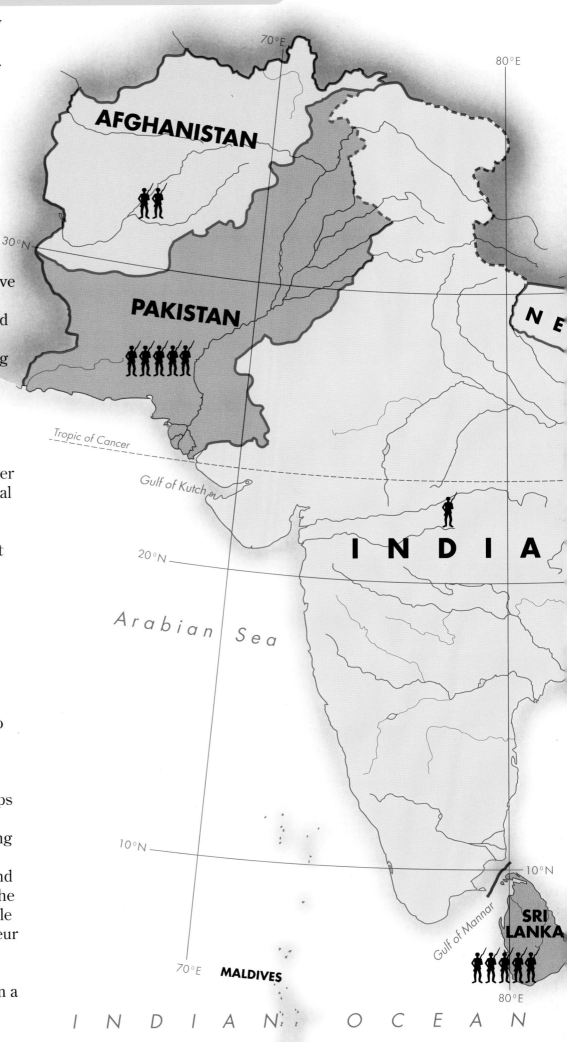

Most terrorist groups fail to achieve their long-range plans. Governments fight terrorists by refusing to give in to their demands, by increasing security at airports and other likely targets, and by developing special forces to rescue hostages.

Main outlets of Terrorism

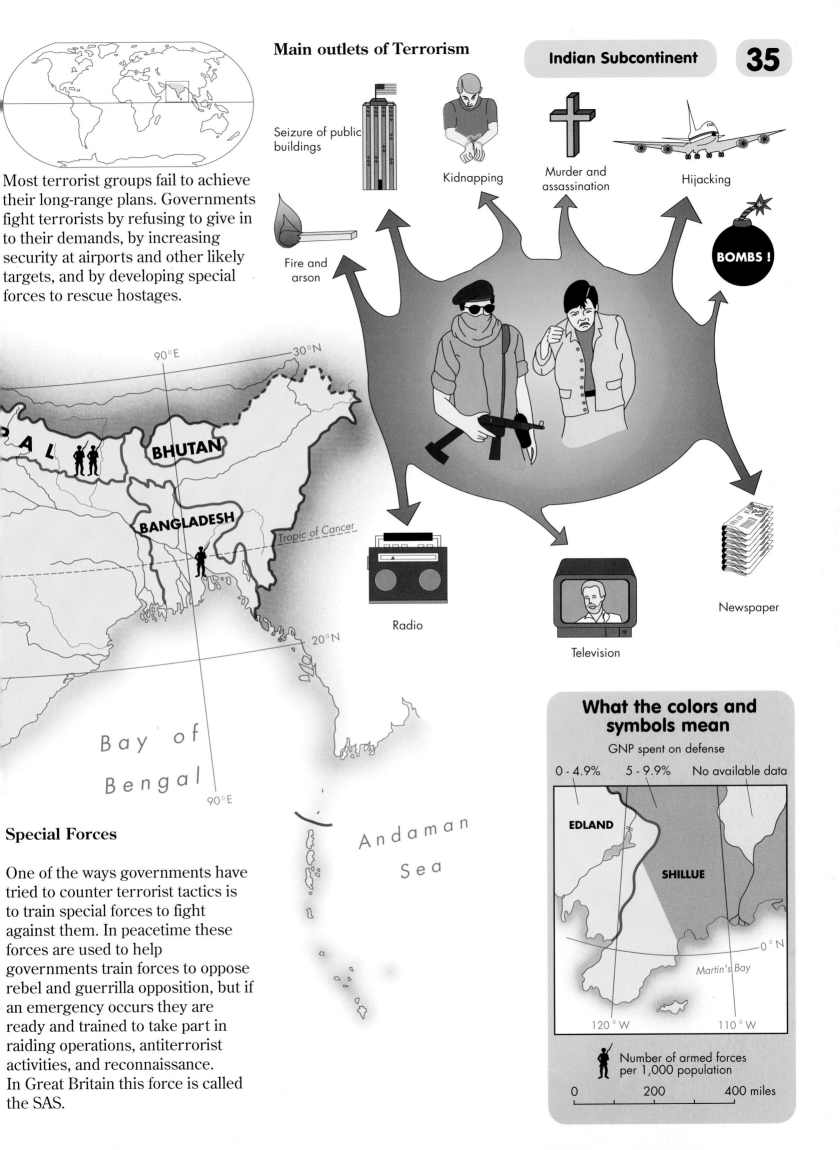

Seizure of public buildings

Kidnapping

Murder and assassination

Hijacking

Fire and arson

BOMBS !

Radio

Television

Newspaper

Special Forces

One of the ways governments have tried to counter terrorist tactics is to train special forces to fight against them. In peacetime these forces are used to help governments train forces to oppose rebel and guerrilla opposition, but if an emergency occurs they are ready and trained to take part in raiding operations, antiterrorist activities, and reconnaissance. In Great Britain this force is called the SAS.

BHUTAN

BANGLADESH

Tropic of Cancer

Bay of Bengal

Andaman Sea

90°E · 30°N

20°N

90°E

What the colors and symbols mean

GNP spent on defense

0 - 4.9%   5 - 9.9%   No available data

EDLAND

SHILLUE

Martin's Bay

0°N

120°W   110°W

Number of armed forces per 1,000 population

0   200   400 miles

The aftermath of the Gulf War still finds the Middle East far from peaceful. Conflict between Israel and its Arab neighbors continues. The rebuilding of Lebanon, after a lengthy civil war, has only just begun, and Iraq is still the scene of bitter revolts by the Kurdish minorities in the north and the Shiite rebels in the south.

The Gulf War

Iraq invaded Kuwait on August 2, 1990. The invasion took 6 hours to complete, and there was fear that Iraqi forces would continue southward into Saudi Arabia. The Arab League proved to be divided, though it condemned the invasion.

The USA reacted swiftly, and its first forces were deployed to Saudi Arabia on August 7. The United Nations had imposed sanctions on Iraq on August 6.

Over the next six months, there was an impressive buildup of forces — code-named Operation Desert Shield. U.S. personnel were joined by ground and air forces from France and the UK and ground forces from a number of Arab and Muslim countries. Eventually there were troops from 29 countries deployed in the Gulf.

The UN authorized the use of "all necessary means" to regain Kuwait if Iraq did not withdraw from Kuwait by midnight on January 15, 1991. Iraq did not comply, and Operation Desert Storm began on January 17. Some five weeks later a massive ground offensive was launched, and a cease-fire was ordered 100 hours later on February 28.

In Iraq the end of the war was followed by uprisings of the Shiites in the south and the Kurds in the north. Both were ruthlessly crushed by the remains of the Iraqi Army. The Shiites fled to Iran and the marshland southeast of Basra; the Kurds fled to the mountainous Iraq-Turkey-Iran borders.

Coalition forces kept out of these uprisings for a while, until public pressure forced them to deploy a new allied force to establish safe havens for Kurdish refugees.

Chemical Warfare

The greatest number of people killed by chemical warfare was an estimated 4,000, who died at Halabja in Iraq in March 1988 when President Saddam Hussein used chemical weapons against Iraq's Kurdish minority for the support they had given to Iran in the Iran-Iraq War.

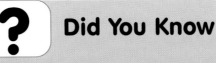

Did You Know

★ The total number of sorties (individual missions) flown by Allied pilots during the Gulf War numbered 110,000.

★ The cost of damage to Kuwait following the Gulf War has been estimated at $30 billion.

League of Arab States

Formed in 1945 and inspired by the Arab awakening of the 19th century, this movement sought to regroup and reintegrate the Arab community.

Members: Algeria, Bahrain, Djibouti, Egypt, Iraq, Jordan, Kuwait, Lebanon, Libya, Mauritania, Morocco, Oman, Palestine Liberation Organization, Qatar, Saudi Arabia, Somalia, Sudan, Syria, Tunisia, United Arab Emirates, and Yemen.

An example of long-range artillery used by Allied Forces against Iraq in the Gulf War.

Caspian Sea

60°E — 40°N

I R A N

30°N

BAHRAIN

QATAR — Gulf

Gulf of Oman

UNITED ARAB EMIRATES

Tropic of Cancer

60°E

OMAN

20°N

Although the commander is in his hatch and the driver is visible, in action both would be concealed and use a periscope for viewing.

Aden

50°E

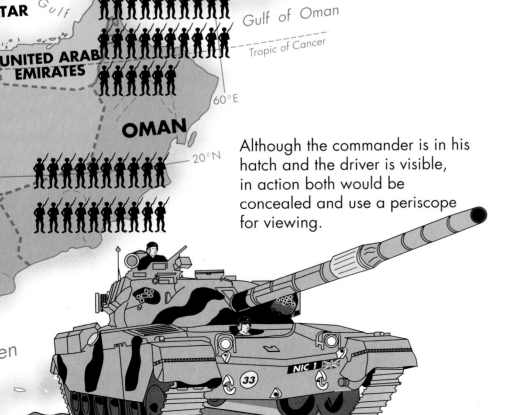

What the colors and symbols mean

GNP spent on defense

| 0 - 4.9% | 5 - 9.9% | 50 %+ |

EDLAND

SHILLUE

0° N

Martin's Bay

120° W   110° W

No available data   10 - 24.9%   25 - 49.9%

Number of armed forces per 1,000 population

Member of NATO

0   200   400 miles

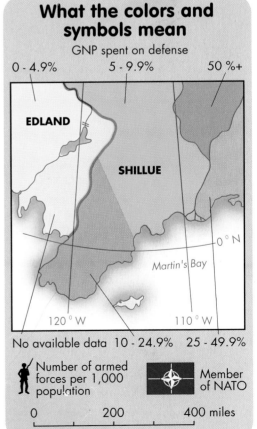

The ANZUS security treaty was signed in 1951 to coordinate defense of the Pacific islands by the United States, Australia, and New Zealand, but New Zealand's decision to ban ships carrying nuclear weapons from its ports in 1985 led to the end of this military pact.

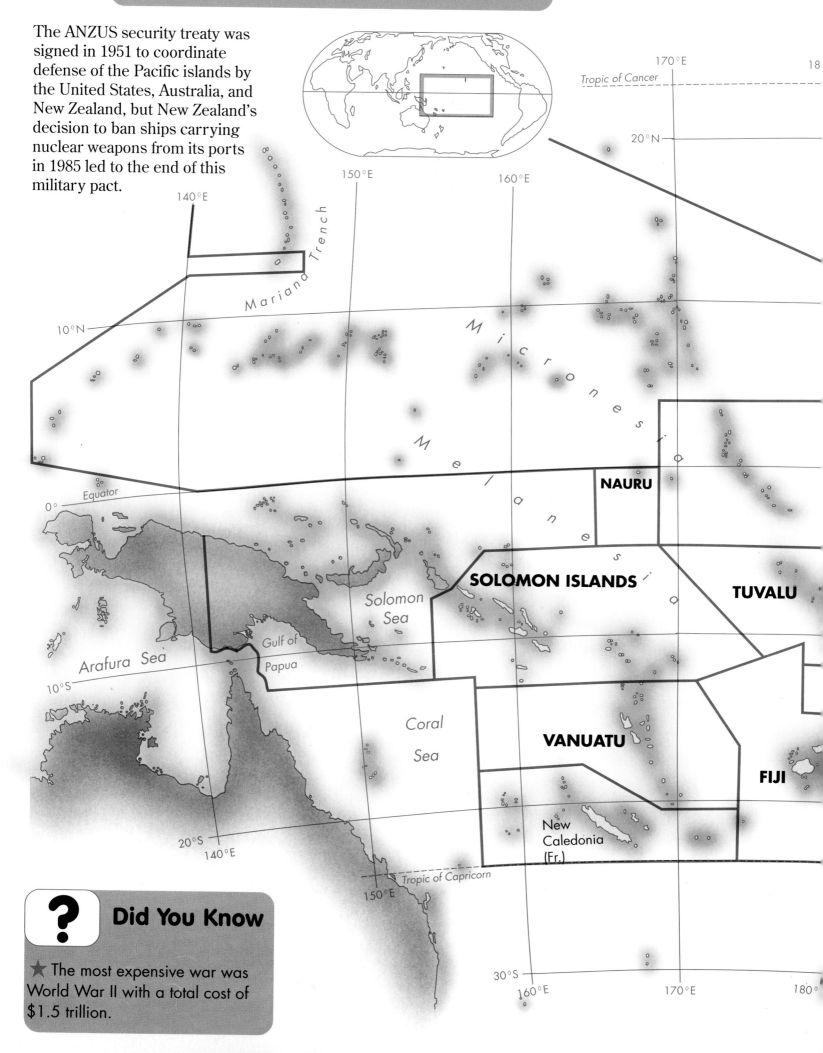

? Did You Know

★ The most expensive war was World War II with a total cost of $1.5 trillion.

What the colors and symbols mean

GNP spent on defense

0 - 4.9   5 - 9.9%

EDLAND

SHILLUE

Martin's Bay

120° W   110° W

0° N

No available data

| 0 | 200 | 400 | 600 miles |

160° W   150° W

Tropic of Cancer

20° N

*Hawaii
(U.S.)*

10° N

Occupied Pacific Islands World War II

Kiribati		until 1943 then	
Nauru		until 1945 then	
Papua New Guinea		until 1945 then	
Solomon Islands		until 1943 then	

Japanese Defeats World War II

Coral Sea	May 1942
Midway Island	June 1942
Guadalcanal	Winter 1942 - Spring 1943
Leyte	October 1944
Okinawa	April - June 1945

170° W

PACIFIC

Line Islands

Equator

0°

KIRIBATI

OCEAN

P o l y n e s i a

WESTERN SAMOA

TONGA

130° W

10° S

20° S

Tropic of Capricorn

130° W

170° W

160° W

150° W   30° S

140° W

Without question the strongest and most technologically advanced military power, the United States has emerged from the Gulf War with great credit. The end of the Warsaw Pact and the success of arms limitations talks between the superpowers is a source of hope for the future.

Strategic Defense Initiative (SDI) or "Star Wars"

SDI is the name given to the U.S. effort to develop an active defense against nuclear missiles. The system involves the use of high-technology weapons mounted on satellites in outer space. These would include lasers and other devices capable of destroying missiles and warheads in flight. This is a very controversial development for a number of reasons.

The main objection is the huge amount of money needed to create even a partial system. Many of the technologies needed to actually complete the SDI system are only in the developmental stages. Many critics agree that it would only provoke other nations to develop a system to counteract SDI, and so the arms race would continue.

On the other hand, there are those who argue that nuclear aggression is most likely when the attacking nation believes it can win and destroy the other nation in a first strike. SDI supporters believe that even a partial system would be effective in undermining this belief.

The success of Patriot missiles in defense of targets in Saudi Arabia and Israel during the Gulf War has given a boost to SDI. Recently there has been a change of focus away from the defense of US territory against an all-out missile attack, toward the protection of US allies and their forces overseas from accidental, unauthorized, and limited ballistic missile attack. The new system is called Global Protection Against Limited Strikes (GPALS).

The Star Wars system

Second attack

Missile attacked by laser

Satellite sends information to 5 about any remaining warheads

Laser attack

Launched missile is tracked by satellite

The Star Wars system would attack missiles at different stages during their flight

Infrared probe sends information to 7 about any remaining warheads

Attack from earth with non-nuclear devices

ATTACKERS

DEFENDERS

U.S. Rapid Deployment Force

This is a U.S. military force designed to move quickly to protect U.S. interests anywhere around the world. It consists of land, air, and sea units drawn from the Army, Air Force, Marine Corps, and Navy. Units are assembled only when needed. Established in 1980, it was mainly formed to protect U.S. interests in the Middle East, as this region provides much of the oil the U.S. imports.

Amazing - But True

★ The American Civil War was one of the first wars to be photographed.

Navies

Largest in terms of manpower is the U.S. Navy with 590,500 seamen plus 159,300 Marines in 1990. Vessels include 6 nuclear-powered aircraft carriers, 9 other aircraft carriers, 4 battleships, 34 ballistic missile submarines, 90 nuclear attack submarines, 1 diesel attack submarine, 43 cruisers, 59 destroyers, 100 frigates, and 65 amphibious warships.

The former Soviet Union has a larger submarine fleet of 323 vessels, including 63 nuclear attack vessels. It also has 5 aircraft carriers, 43 cruisers, 31 destroyers, 148 frigates, and 77 amphibious warships.

American Deaths in Vietnam

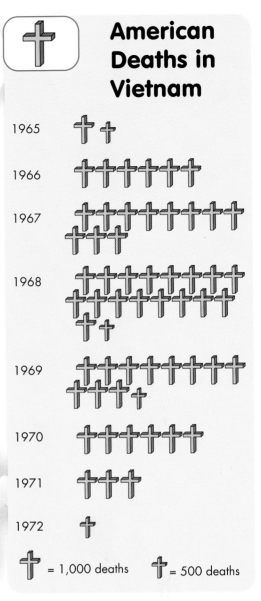

1965

1966

1967

1968

1969

1970

1971

1972

✝ = 1,000 deaths   ✝ = 500 deaths

What the colors and symbols mean

GNP spent on defense
5 - 9.9%

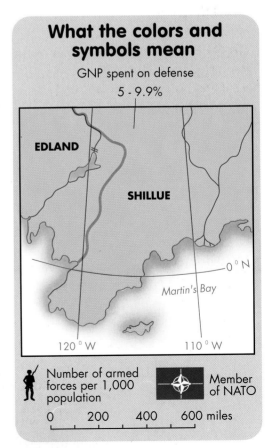

EDLAND

SHILLUE

0° N

Martin's Bay

120° W   110° W

Number of armed forces per 1,000 population

Member of NATO

0   200   400   600 miles

ATLANTIC OCEAN

STATES

AMERICA

Gulf of Mexico

Straits of Florida

Tropic of Cancer

40° N
70° W

30° N

80° W

90° W

100° W

90° W

80° W

Arsenal
A store for arms, ammunition, other weapons and military items.

Biological warfare
The use of living organisms or infectious substances to bring disease or death to humans, animals and plants.

Buffer
A buffer state is a small country that is neutral and exists between two powerful and antagonistic states.

Chemical warfare
The use in war of gaseous, liquid, or solid substances which are intended to have a harmful or even a deadly effect on humans, plants or animals.

Civil War
A war between different interest groups or political groups in the same nation.

Cold war
The hostility between the USA and the former Soviet Union and their respective allies after the second World War was known as the cold war.

Conventional forces
Soldiers armed with non-nuclear weapons.

Court martial
A military court that sits in judgement over charges that martial (military) laws have been broken.

Disengagement
The withdrawal of troops from the scene of a battle or from a close engagement in action.

Guerrilla warfare
The waging of a low-level campaign by unofficial forces against an occupying power or enemy force.

Low-intensity conflict
A US term used to describe its involvements in the Third World.

Monitor
To observe, check, and keep a close record of something.

Neutron bomb
A nuclear weapon that is designed so that it causes little blast or radioactive contamination but destroys all life in the target area.

Nuclear warfare
War involving the use of nuclear weapons. Nuclear weapons now include bombs, missiles, depth charges, and land mines.

Sanction
A measure adopted by a number of states in order to apply pressure to another state that has broken international agreements.

Sovereignty
The power and authority of a state. The absolute authority of a state is its distinguishing feature as a nation differentiating it from any other sort of community.

Tactical nuclear weapons
Shorter-range nuclear weapons, including artillery shells, nuclear mines, torpedoes, and short-range guided missiles.

Terrorists
Political activists who resort to violence. They are also known as urban guerrillas or "freedom fighters" by those who support them.

Theater weapons
Those weapons directed at the immediate battlefield.

Thermonuclear devices
Weapons that get their power from the combining of atomic nuclei under intense heat.

Transgression
A breach of the law or rules.

Truce
A temporary agreement to stop fighting.

Uranium
A radioactive element used in nuclear energy.

Verification
A check or substantiation of the evidence to prove that an assertion is correct.

Violation
An infringement of or disregard for an agreement.

Adelman, Jonathan R. *Revolution, Armies, and War.*
Boulder, CO: Rienner, 1985.

Alger, John I. *Definitions and Doctrine of the Military Art.*
2nd ed. Wayne, NJ: Avery Publishing Group, 1985.

Freedman, Lawrence. *Atlas of Global Strategy.*
New York: Facts on File, 1985.

Harkavy, Robert E, and Stephanie G. Neuman. *The Lessons of Recent Wars in the Third World.*
Lexington MA: Lexington Books, 1985.

Kennedy, Paul M. *The Rise and Fall of the Great Powers.*
New York: Random House, 1988.

Koenig, William J. *Weapons of World War 3.*
New York: Crescent Books, 1981.

Macksey, Kenneth. *The Penguin Encyclopedia of Modern Warfare: 1850 to the Present Day.*
New York: Viking, 1991.

Seabury, Paul. *War.*
New York: Basic Books, 1989.

This index is designed to help you to find places shown on the maps. The index is in alphabetical order and lists all towns, countries, and physical features. After each entry extra information is given to describe the entry and to tell you which country or continent it is in.

The next column contains the latitude and longitude figures. These are used to help locate places on maps. They are measured in degrees. The blue lines drawn across the map are lines of latitude. The equator is at latitude 0°. All lines above the equator are referred to as °N (north of the equator). All lines below the equator are referred to as °S (south of the equator).

The blue lines drawn from the top to the bottom of the map are lines of longitude. The 0° line passes through Greenwich, London, and is known as the Greenwich Meridian. All lines of longitude join the North Pole to the South Pole. All lines to the right of the Greenwich Meridian are referred to as °E (east of Greenwich), and all lines to the left of the Greenwich Meridian are referred to as °W (west of Greenwich).

The final column indicates the number of the page where you will find the place for which you are searching.

If you want to find out where the Gulf of Thailand is, look it up in the alphabetical index. The entry will read:

Name, Description	Location		Page
	Lat.	Long.	
Thailand, Gulf of, Asia	11°N	101°E	22

Turn to page 22 in your atlas. The Gulf of Thailand is located where latitude 11°N meets longitude 101°E. Place a pencil along latitude 11°N. Now take another pencil and place it along 101°E. Where the two pencils meet is the location of the Gulf of Thailand. Practice finding places in the index and on the maps.

Name, Description	Location		Page
	Lat.	Long.	
A			
Aden, Gulf of, Middle East	12°N	47°E	36
Adriatic Sea, Europe	43°N	15°E	33
Afghanistan, country in Asia	33°N	65°E	34
Alaska, Gulf of, North America	59°N	145°W	40
Albania, country in Europe	41°N	20°E	31
Algeria, country in Africa	25°N	0°	10
Andaman Sea, Indian Ocean	11°N	96°E	35
Andorra, country in Europe	43°N	2°E	32
Angola, country in Africa	12°S	18°E	12
Antigua and Barbuda, island country in Caribbean Sea	18°N	62°W	15
Arabian Sea, Indian Ocean	15°N	65°E	34
Arafura Sea, Southeast Asia	9°S	135°E	24
Aral Sea, in Asia	45°N	60°E	28
Argentina, country in South America	40°S	68°W	17
Australia, continent and country	23°S	135°E	24

Name, Description	Location		Page
	Lat.	Long.	
Austria, country in Europe	48°N	15°E	33
B			
Baffin Bay, North America	72°N	65°W	27
Bahamas, island country in Atlantic Ocean	25°N	78°W	15
Bahrain, country in Middle East	26°N	51°E	37
Baltic Sea, Europe	57°N	19°E	31
Bangladesh, country in Asia	23°N	90°E	35
Barbados, island country in Caribbean Sea	13°N	59°W	15
Barents Sea, Arctic Ocean	73°N	35°E	28
Bass Strait, Australia	40°S	146°E	25
Beaufort Sea, Arctic Ocean	73°N	140°W	26
Belgium, country in Europe	51°N	5°E	32
Belize, country in Central America	17°N	89°W	14
Bellingshausen Sea, Antarctica	67°S	85°W	18
Bengal, Bay of, Indian Ocean	19°N	89°E	35
Benin, country in Africa	10°N	2°E	10
Bering Sea, Pacific Ocean	60°N	175°W	40

Scott E. Morris is an associate professor of geography at the University of Idaho where his current areas of teaching and research interest include mountain geomorphology, field methods, and human impact on the landscape process. Dr. Morris received his Ph.D. from the University of Colorado, Boulder and is published prolifically on the formation and climatic history of mountain landscapes, the effects of wildfire and mineral resource extraction on soil erosion processes, and the influence of water diversion and channel modification on sediment transport.